A Penguin Special
The European Parliament

Robert Jackson is a former Fellow of All Souls College, Oxford, and an ex-President of the Oxford Union. He has spent four years working in the Community institutions in Brussels, where he was a member of the *Cabinet* of Sir Christopher Soames – now Lord Soames – at the Commission, and *Chef de Cabinet* to the President of the Economic and Social Committee, Mr Basil de Ferranti. He is a former editor of *The Round Table: The Commonwealth Journal of International Affairs* and the author of *South Asian Crisis: The India-Pakistan-Bangladesh War of 1971*. He is at present working on a study of European defence. In 1974, after serving as Political Secretary to Mr William Whitelaw at the Department of Employment, he stood as a Conservative candidate in Manchester.

John Fitzmaurice read politics and economics at Bristol University and has done postgraduate work at Oxford, Brussels and Bristol, including a study of the role of national parliaments in Community affairs. Since 1973 he has been a principal administrator in the Secretariat of the European Commission in Brussels, dealing with relations between the Commission and the European Parliament. He is the author of *The Party Groups in the European Parliament* (1975).

Mr Jackson is an active member of the Conservative Party and Mr Fitzmaurice is an active member of the Labour Party.

Robert Jackson
and John Fitzmaurice

The European Parliament

A Guide for the
European Elections

Penguin Books

Penguin Books Ltd, Harmondsworth,
Middlesex, England
Penguin Books, 625 Madison Avenue,
New York, New York 10022, U.S.A.
Penguin Books Australia Ltd, Ringwood,
Victoria, Australia
Penguin Books Canada Ltd, 2801 John Street,
Markham, Ontario, Canada L3R 1B4
Penguin Books (N.Z.) Ltd, 182–190 Wairau Road,
Auckland 10, New Zealand

First published 1979

Copyright © Robert Jackson and John Fitzmaurice, 1979

Made and printed in Great Britain by
Hazell Watson & Viney Ltd, Aylesbury, Bucks
Set in VIP Plantin

For CFJ
and BJW

Contents

Preface

And he said unto me,
'Son of Man, can these bones live?'

Ezekiel xxxvii, 3

Remember that time and habit are at least as
necessary to fix the true character of
government as of other human institutions.

*George Washington's
Farewell Address, 1796*

Preface

This book is intended as background reading for European citizens reflecting on the significance of their vote in European direct elections, and concerned to understand more fully the character of the Parliament to which they will for the first time be electing representatives. It attempts to fill a gap – to provide a short, factual guide to this new political phenomenon, viewed both in a British and in a wider Community perspective.

The authors are of course aware that there is an abundance of academic writing both on the European Parliament and on the European elections – indeed they have both already contributed to it. This book has no pretensions to rival this perhaps rather specialized literature. Both authors, however, came independently to the view that there was room for a brief guide in paperback format to the background of direct elections. In this they felt that their differing experience and party allegiance could be complementary; and indeed Robert Jackson was more particularly responsible for Chapters 1, 2, 3 and 6, and John Fitzmaurice for Chapters 4 and 5.

This book does not enter into the controversy about whether direct elections should or should not take place. It takes as its starting point the fact that they will be held in June 1979. In this connection it is right that the authors should make clear the perspective from which they have written. Although they recognize the seriousness of the reservations of those who are opposed to further European integration, they consider that the growth of the Community towards closer unity is a necessary pragmatic response to the problems which Western Europe faces – which are in many cases trans-national in character. And they also believe that it is a work of high moral and spiritual significance for its own sake. The challenge is to find forms of organization and democratic processes which respect national identity but which also assure a sufficient concentration of power at the European level to make possible an effective response to the difficult issues of the coming period.

What form this organization will eventually take is not yet clear. Yet, whatever the 'final' shape of the European Union, it will surely both embody the heritage of the present Community and also be marked decisively by the issues and opportunities it will have met in the course of its evolution. Some of these issues are already with us – unemployment, inflation, economic divergence, the trans-national scale of business, pressures both economic and political from the world outside Europe, the prospect of the enlargement of the Community to include Greece, Portugal and Spain. We do not yet know how the Community will respond to the opportunities which these challenges represent. But the authors believe that the first European elections will afford an important opportunity for them to be discussed.

On these wider issues this book offers no answers – otherwise it would be a different book. Here the authors' purpose is simply to assist judgement in these matters by explaining as clearly and objectively as possible the main factors, both negative and positive, that will affect the European Parliament and its future role.

The authors would like to record their thanks to Miss Marylyn Holmes, who had the patience to 'decode' the original manuscript and turn it into a clean typescript. They would like to acknowledge the help at various stages and in varying degrees of: G. E. Andrews, Tom Arnold, MP, I. du V. Arnol Davies, Timothy Bainbridge, Tim Boswell, Mrs I. A. Channon, J. Davies, Basil de Ferranti, Emmanuel Gazzo, R. W. Gellatly, Miss L. Green, David Hannay, Donald Hardie, John Harvey, Richard Hay, V. Herman, Mrs L. F. Higginson, Stuart Laing, John Lee, P. Lee-Roberts, G. Leon-Smith, Eberhard Loerke, M. Lowry, David Marquand, R. Martin, Stephen Milligan, C. Nisser, Riccardo Perissich, C. T. Pertwee, Dr and Mrs G. Pridham, Julian Priestley, Geoffrey Rippon, MP, John Roper, MP, J.-J. Schwed, Peter Thring, Geoffrey Tucker, I. J. Wallace, G. B. Wood, F. Woods.

The views expressed in this book are, of course, the authors' own exclusive reponsibility.

Chapter 1: A European Election

On the morning of Thursday 7 June 1979, polling-stations throughout the British Isles will open for a new kind of election. But although it will be new, much will be familiar. The physical setting will be almost the same as in other elections; the same empty echoing rooms in which footsteps sound loud among the whispers; the same church halls and primary schools, the same tin boxes and rough-and-ready folding screens. Behind the tables, handing out the voting papers, there will be the same local authority staff; the ballot papers themselves will look the same, offering the usual variety of candidates and a space to put one's cross. Outside at the doors, there will be the same tellers from the local Labour Party, the Conservative Association, the Liberals; on the street outside the same kind of posters urging the merits of 'X', the Tory candidate, and 'Y', the Labour man.

Though so much will be familiar, in one fundamental respect the election will be different from any held in Britain before: 175 million Europeans from the north of Scotland to Calabria in Italy, from the Bay of Biscay to the Elbe, will be voting together, over the next four days, in a single election.[1] Indeed, when polling is finished in Britain on Thursday night, the verified ballots will be locked away until the count takes place on Sunday night or Monday morning, after voting is complete all over the Community. Announcement of the British results on television and radio –

1. Voting will not be confined to the geographical limits of Western Europe. As part of Denmark, Greenland will be electing a Member to the European Parliament. And electors in the French overseas *départements* in the Caribbean, the South Pacific and the Indian Ocean will be voting on the French national list. In Britain Commonwealth citizens will be eligible to vote and to stand as candidates: there is therefore at least a possibility of some Australians, New Zealanders, Canadians or Indians being elected to the European Parliament.

15

David Butler will be there as usual – will be interspersed with results from France, from Germany, from Italy. Interest will centre not only on the performance of the parties in Britain, but also on what has happened all over the Nine – because for the first time an election in Britain will not be complete in itself, but will be part of a wider process which will not be terminated until the last vote has been cast and counted over the whole Community.

For though British voters will have been among the first to vote, all over the Community in the four days after 7 June the same experience of something both familiar yet also quite novel and different will have been repeated. For the first time the entire adult population of most of Western Europe will have been eligible to vote in an election to a Europe-wide representative assembly. Thirty-five years ago the men and women, and their fathers and mothers, now casting their votes as fellow-Europeans in this first-ever European election were at each other's throats, locked in deadly and – so it seemed at the time – irreconcilable conflict. In Normandy almost to the day of the thirty-fifth anniversary of 'D-Day' there will be French men and women casting their votes as Europeans in rooms which echoed not so long ago to the very different sounds of guns firing and men dying. On this June week-end, the outlines of a new democratic European politics will have begun to take shape – a democratic European Community larger than the United States and second only to India in numbers.

The *outlines* of a new democratic European politics . . . Among the hundred million and more Europeans who will be putting their cross on the ballot paper in those June days there will be many who will remember the war, or who will otherwise feel the historical weight of that moment. But as they reflect upon the significance of their vote they will nevertheless be able to see little more than the embryonic form of the European Community to whose future life and growth their participation will be contributing.

For although it will be clear that these are *European* elections, invested with a profound importance for the future of the European Community as such, there is also no doubt that local and national considerations will loom so large in the foreground as to obscure from many the European perspectives that lie beyond.

The electoral system will differ from country to country according to national tradition and preference[2]; the elections will be contested by candidates and political parties whose identity is essentially national; the communications media through which they reach out to their electorates will be almost exclusively national and local; and in each country there will be pressing local and national issues which will help to shape the way in which electors vote.

The Electoral Systems

First – the electoral systems. The fact that different systems will be used in each country will tend to fragment the election into national segments. The distribution of seats has been decided at the European level: Britain, France, Germany and Italy will have 81 each, Holland will have 25, Belgium 24, Denmark 16, Ireland 15 and Luxembourg 6. But within this broad European framework – which also includes, for example, the requirement of universal adult suffrage – the choice of electoral system in the first round of European elections has been left to the Community's member states.[3] Inevitably their decision reflects differences in national experiences and national political circumstances, with the result that most of the systems that have been chosen are adaptations or variants of the familiar national elections systems. Only in France is there a major departure from the established national system.

The electoral systems around which the European elections in June will be organized are, broadly, of three different types: (1) the national party list; (2) the regional party list; (3) the single-Member constituency system.

2. See Appendix B, p. 162.

3. Member states have also been left free to decide what to do about their residents who are nationals of other Community countries. Ireland has given a vote to all Community citizens living there; the Netherlands will give a vote to Community citizens living there who have no vote elsewhere; Danes and Germans living in other Community countries may vote at home in the European election – which they cannot do in national elections. Britain has decided not to give a vote to its nationals living elsewhere in the Community.

National list systems. National lists will be used in France, the Netherlands, Luxembourg and Denmark. In Germany the political parties have the option of presenting either a single national list or lists on a *Land* basis; however, in the distribution of seats between parties it will be the share of the national vote as a whole that will count. Each party will get the same proportion of seats as it gets of the vote.

In France voters will not be able to choose between candidates of the same party – they will simply vote for a list in which the order of names has been decided by the parties. In the other countries using the national list system voters will to a greater or lesser extent be able to influence which candidates from each party list are elected.

Regional list systems. Regional lists will be used in Belgium, Ireland and Italy. As under the national list system, the seats each party gets will be proportionate to the votes cast for it; but the electors will vote on a regional rather than a national basis.

In Belgium there will be two regions, the Walloon (French-speaking) with 11 seats and the Flemish with 13 seats. Brussels voters will be able to choose in which region they prefer to vote. In Italy at the time of writing no decision had been taken as to the number of regions, but it is expected that they will group together existing administrative regions into four, five or six large regional constituencies. In Ireland there will be three, four or five seat constituencies corresponding to the ancient Irish Provinces; and the single transferable vote method will be used.

The single-Member constituency system. The 'first past the post' single-Member constituency system will be used in Britain and in Greenland (whose one Member will be part of the Danish delegation). Northern Ireland will, however, be an exception in Britain – it will be treated as a single regional constituency electing three Members with a single transferable vote. In England, Scotland and Wales the Westminster constituencies have been grouped together, seven or eight to each European constituency, thus giving every part of each country an identifiable Member to represent it in the EP.

Of the 81 seats allocated to the United Kingdom, England will have 66, with an average electorate of 514,067. Scotland will have 8 (an average electorate of 470,399); and Wales will have 4 (average 344,413). A novel feature of the European elections will be that peers will be able both to vote and to stand for election.

It is inevitable that these differences in the electoral system will lead to variations in the way in which the various member states respond to direct elections. The deepest difference in this respect will be that between Britain, with its single-Member constituency system, and the continental countries and Ireland using various forms of proportional representation.

PR has the effect at the national level of making it easier for small parties to achieve representation. This will also happen in the European elections, in which the familiar national parties will all be presenting candidates. There will, however, be some differences from the pattern at national elections. Some small parties in Italy and Denmark may fight in alliance. Other parties in countries with many parties – Italy, Netherlands, Denmark – may not enter the lists at all. In Denmark, at least, a new political force will enter upon the scene – the Peoples' Movement against the EEC – which might win some seats. In Germany and France the so-called 'Green Lists' of 'ecological' candidates may make some headway. And even in Britain it is probable that the novelty of the occasion will attract a richer than normal crop of 'independent' candidates – for example, Lord George-Brown has indicated that he intends to stand.

The continental delegations are likely, therefore, to contain a larger number of parties than are likely to achieve representation in Britain. Indeed it is probable that no British Liberals will be returned and that outside Northern Ireland all the seats will be divided between the Conservative and Labour parties.

Another important possible effect of this difference in electoral systems between Britain and the continent could be that it may produce national delegations of markedly different quality.

In the continental countries using the list system it will be easier than in Britain for the parties to ensure the return of a balanced set of candidates with a suitable range of European expertise. Similarly the list systems – which do not involve onerous constituency responsibilities – will be used on the continent to return a number of very senior party figures, for example Willy Brandt and François Mitterand. It is also probable that on the continent the candidates for the EP will for the most part resemble their counterparts at the national level, both in background and in terms of the spread of age between 'young turks' and 'old foxes'. In Britain, however, the result may be less satisfactorily balanced. The fact that we will be using a constituency system will probably lead the selection committees to attach considerable importance to practical experience in fighting elections; but for many politicians the decision whether or not to put themselves forward will be a very difficult one. Being a member both of the EP and at Westminster will be almost impossible to manage for politicians not standing on a list system, even though the so-called 'dual mandate' will be permitted in every member state. And there is a risk that in Britain the problem may be met, if not solved, by choosing large numbers of retired people who have reached the end of their careers at Westminster, or elsewhere, and who may not fully appreciate the demands that the new EP – not to mention the large British Euro-constituencies – will make on their time and energies.

The Role of the Parties

Amid the novelty of the European elections the most familiar factor will be the political parties contesting them. They will have a crucial role to play in helping the electors make the connection between their familiar national politics and the new European politics.

The parties' first task will be the selection of candidates. In Britain this will be done, probably in the first two months of 1979, by European constituency organizations set up by linking the local parties and associations of the seven of eight Westminster constituencies which have been grouped together in each European division. These organizations will choose candidates in the usual way – normally concluding at a meeting representative of all the local party executives. And they will establish the machinery which is required to help the candidates nurse and fight the constituency, and run it if he wins.

The comparatively large size of the European constituencies will present challenges. These should not, however, be overestimated. The European divisions will be not very much larger than the electoral districts of the United States House of Representatives; and American experience suggests that is it perfectly possible to run large constituencies with half a million electors at least as effectively – if not more so – as the smaller-scale Westminster division with an average of 60,000 electors.

The main problem – as usual – will be that of finance. Like American Congressmen, the Members of the European Parliament are likely to be given some supporting staff paid for by the Parliament – but not on the same lavish scale as Congress. So paying for the running of the new European constituencies will not present the financial difficulties that Westminster constituency parties and associations must face. On the other hand, unless the British government decides, under Labour Party pressure, to provide British public funds for the campaign, its cost will, as usual, have to be met by the parties both locally and nationally.

National public funds will, of course, pay for the administrative costs of the election – they will be about the same as in a general election – and for the free postal distribution of some party literature. This is normal practice in Britain. A new feature will be that funds from the Community budget will also be available to the parties in the pre-campaign period. Although at the time of writing the budget for next year had not yet been adopted, it is likely that a substantial amount of money, of the order of £6 million, will be given to the Parliament's Party Groups for information and other specified activities. Of this, about 30 per cent will be allocated to the Socialist Group and about 9 per cent to the Conservative Group. The Groups will then have to decide how to divide this money among their constituent parties; and these parties will in turn have to consider how it should be spent at the national level. In the

event Conservative Central Office and Transport House will probably each receive several hundred thousand pounds from the Community budget to spend on preparatory information for the
European elections. But the local party organizations will probably
have to raise for themselves the bulk of the funds to pay for their
local campaigns – on which the overall limit in each British Euro-
constituency is likely to be in the order of £15,000 for each candidate.[4]

Where will this money come from? In Britain, with a general
election falling within six months of the European election, it may
not be possible for some local parties to finance these efforts in the
traditional way from funds accumulated over several years' saving
from subscriptions, and money-raising drives. There is a risk that
some of them may take the easy way out and look for candidates –
if such there may be – able and willing to pay for the election
themselves. Another risk is that the parties will simply decide to
spend as little as possible. What is perhaps to be hoped is that, just
as the large size of the constituencies will require new campaign
techniques to be applied, so the need for new sources of finance
will lead to new thinking. In Britain, unlike America, there is very
little direct sponsorship of candidates by organizations other than
political parties and trade unions: corporate money normally goes
to parties rather than to candidates, and other interest and public
action groups tend to hold themselves aloof. The European elections may lead to a review of this policy – with important possible
implications not only for the European elections but also eventually for national politics.

Candidate-selection, fund-raising, local organization – all this
will follow tried and tested experience. And the fact that all the
Community's political parties have an essentially national – as
opposed to European – identity will inevitably confirm the char-

4. A government White Paper published in August 1978 – and likely to be
accepted by the opposition parties – proposes a limit of £5,000 plus 2p for each
registered elector – that is to say about £15,000 per constituency. The proposed
deposit is £600; nomination papers, it is suggested, should be subscribed by thirty
electors.

acter of the campaign as a set of separate national elections with a European dimension.

Nevertheless, as we shall see in Chapter 5, in most countries the main parties will belong to one of the three European Party Organizations – the Confederation of Socialist Parties in the European Community, the European Peoples' Party (the Christian Democrats) and the Federation of Liberal and Democratic Parties of the Community. The British Conservative Party belongs to a looser grouping of the centre-right; and the Communist parties, though members of no formal European Party Organization, will no doubt make something of the Europe-wide dimensions of their movement. These European Party Organizations are largely embryonic. They lack authority, staff and finance, and their manifestos are still rudimentary and highly generalized. But symbolically they will be very important because they provide a point of reference for their member parties and a framework within which the campaign can be given a European flavour – for example by bringing leaders on highly publicized visits from one country to another. More than anything else it will be the existence of these links with parties in other Community countries which will differentiate the European elections from other sorts of national election.

The Issues

One of the main differences between a national election and the European campaign will be that the issues will be different, that they will often be new, and usually more complex.

Of course, the parties contesting the election will be seen by the vast majority of electors in almost exclusively national terms. They will therefore attract support on the basis of their established national identity rather than their European policies; and their primary appeal to their supporters will be in terms of party loyalty. There will consequently be a tendency for the European election to become more of a test of the strength of the parties in national terms than a debate about European issues.

Indeed in some countries the significance of the European election will be seen mainly in terms of its possible effects on the domestic political scene. In France it is expected to be an important influence on the standing of the rival parties as they begin the run-up to the Presidential election of 1981. And in Northern Ireland the Rev. Ian Paisley apparently hopes to use the occasion to mark out his position as the leading figure on the Protestant side of politics.

Where the European election seems to have some direct relevance to domestic politics it is probable that the turn-out will be as high as it normally is in national elections. But what about those countries – including Britain – in which the link with national politics is less strong?

So far, the opinion polls indicate that there is in every Community country a strong intention to vote. In the original six member states and in Ireland this is usually associated with pro-European convictions: between 55 and 60 per cent of those asked in those countries feel that the 'Common Market is a good thing', with only about 5 per cent taking the opposite view and some 35 per cent 'don't knows' (poll taken in spring 1978). In Britain and Denmark, on the other hand, the pattern has normally been for opinion to be fairly evenly divided – about 33 per cent each – between 'pros', 'cons' and 'don't knows'. Nevertheless, on the holding of direct elections there is a powerful majority in favour in every Community country, ranging from 54 per cent in favour (22 per cent against) in Denmark to 82 per cent in favour (11 per cent against) in Luxembourg, with 65 per cent in favour in Britain and 17 per cent against. Perhaps the feeling that the Community needs reform in many significant respects may help to ensure an adequate turn-out in Britain and Denmark, just as the feeling that the Community needs to be strengthened will play its part in the other member states.

During the election much time will have to be spent by candidates and parties explaining what the Community is, what powers the European Parliament has and might acquire, what the significance of direct elections is, and what he or she would hope to achieve as an MEP. Candidates will also have to explain the fact that the purpose of the election is not to elect a government, and that the area covered by the Community's responsibilities – and therefore those of the Parliament – is limited in scope. This may be another factor affecting turn-out. On the continent the limited role of the EP may be better understood because the idea of the separation of powers and the limited functions of the legislature is more familiar than it is in Britain. There is a danger that on this side of the Channel some electors may feel that it is not worth voting in elections for any parliament with less ambitious claims than those of Westminster.

There should not, however, be any shortage of subjects for debate in the European election campaign. These will range from the trivial to the sublime.

Amongst the former must surely be classed the arguments which are likely to rage in some countries – including Britain – about the salaries of European Members. At the time of writing this matter had not yet been decided.[5] But it is clear that the European scale is going to be considerably higher than that on which some national parliamentarians are paid. This question will probably be settled before the elections take place, so with any luck it is likely to be to some extent 'defused' as a campaign issue.

On a higher level of argument, in Britain and Denmark the question whether or not the country's membership of the Community is desirable will still be an issue – although this is bound to turn increasingly into that different question which will in fact be at issue everywhere in the election, of *what sort* of Community the electorate want to see developing in the future. Should the Community develop towards economic and monetary union, and in

5. Appendix D (pp. 167–71) sets out the very different levels of salaries and allowances in the various member state parliaments. Clearly it would not be politically sensible to pay British or Irish MEPs the same as German parliamentarians. But there do exist ways of paying all MEPs the same *in purchasing power terms* while giving them different rates *in money terms*. Furthermore, the salaries may be subject to national taxation. The net income of MEPs in Britain might not therefore seem excessive: but it is bound to be bigger than that of MPs at Westminster – even after the rise they are likely to get after the general election. On the other hand, readers of this book will be able to judge for themselves whether a high rate is not appropriate to the job of an MEP, which will involve so much travel, with consequent separation from family and loss of opportunities for extra-parliamentary employment.

what shape or form? Should the Community budget be larger, and if so how should its revenues be increased and to what objects should increased spending be directed? How much transfer of resources from the richer regions of the Community to the poorer should there be? Should the Community develop into the fields of security policy and defence? Should the European Parliament be given new powers? What should be the Community's policy in international trade matters – protectionism or not? How much interventionism in industrial policy should the Community sponsor or undertake itself? What should be done about the Common Agricultural Policy? What about the Common Fisheries Policy? Should the Community develop a binding code of conduct for multinational companies? What policy should be pursued on national state aids to industry, such as the British Temporary Employment Subsidy? Should the Community promote nuclear energy? These are all issues which are central to the future; and they are also all subjects in relation to which the Community, and therefore the European Parliament, is likely to acquire an increasing measure of influence.

Even more interestingly, they are also issues which cut across party lines, causing divisions of opinion which are not so much *between* parties as *within* them. This will probably have the unfortunate effect of blurring their articulation; but on the other hand, if conditioned party reflexes are seen to be inappropriate, the effect could be to bring the issues themselves into sharper focus – with beneficial results for the quality of political debate in Britain. Some electors will find it challenging to hear different candidates of the same party expressing different views about, say, economic and monetary union or European defence. Others will simply be bewildered. But only the party leaderships will find it distressing.

In exploring these issues – and the divisions they provoke – a crucial role will be played by the communications media. For them – especially for television and radio – the European election is likely to be a very stimulating occasion, offering considerable scope for ingenuity and innovation, especially in bringing home its European dimension. Collaborative arrangements between the different national television and radio networks are currently being negotiated, with the BBC taking a lead. At the constituency level the local press and radio stations will have an even bigger role to play than they usually do in national elections. Indeed it could be said that while the parties and the candidates will depend heavily on the media to put their difficult new message over, it is also no less true that the European election will be a significant test of the media's educative and informational capabilities.

The Probable Results

Predicting the results of a Europe-wide election under such novel conditions and with so many unknowns must inevitably be a hazardous exercise. However, the specialists concur in expecting that the balance of power in the new and larger Parliament will be little different from that which exists at present. The Socialists will remain the biggest single Group. The Communist Group will increase – especially in view of the use of the proportional national list system in France. But the two left-of-centre Groups together will continue to fall short of the 206 seats needed for an overall majority. The centre-right will remain as fragmented as it is at present, with at least three Groups: the European Peoples' Party, the Liberals and the Conservatives will approximately balance the left. There will be a larger number of Members than at present owing allegiance to none of the major Groups – regional parties like the Scottish Nationalists, the Italian far right, Danish anti-marketeers. In some crucial votes these Members could be vital, but there will in fact be only two viable majority coalitions: between the Socialists and European Peoples' Party, or between the various forces making up a broad centre-right alliance.

It is probably, however, a mistake to think at this stage in terms of formal coalition-building in the European Parliament. As we shall see in the next chapter, there is no European government to support or oppose, and coalitions between Groups would therefore be needed only on such issues as the election of the Parliament's President and other officers. Otherwise, as now, majorities will no doubt tend to form and dissolve from issue to issue, even across party lines. In this respect, as in so many, the pattern of politics in the EP will be closer to that of the United States Congress than to that at Westminster.

The most important result of the European election will, however, be this – that after the elections have taken place there will be 410 Members of the European Parliament looking for ways to apply and expand their influence on behalf of the people who elected them, to whom they will be returning five years hence. The implications of this for the Parliment itself and for the system of which it is a part are the principal subject of this book. But before we can begin to understand them we have to acquire a firm grasp of the principles of the Community's system of government.

STOP PRESS

The probable survival of Mr Callaghan's minority Labour government until after the Scottish and Welsh referendums on 1 March 1979 opens up the possibility that the British general election may be held on the same day as the European election. Unless a decision by the Labour government not to join the proposed European Monetary System (EMS) is accompanied by Conservative advocacy of the System – thus bringing the European issue to the fore in national party politics – the probability is that if the two elections are held on the same day the European campaign will not be given much attention in Britain. On the other hand, the turn-out in the European ballot will be more satisfactory, especially on the Labour side.

Chapter 2: The Government of the Community

The quarter-century since the Community began has shown that, like all political systems, it evolves almost as a living organism does. The abstract legal framework laid down in the founding Treaties has come to life; the institutions and organs of the Community have grown and shifted in weight and purpose; and new functions and activities have grown up in response to need and opportunity, both within the Treaty framework and outside it.

The Development of the Community System

It is not, however, too mechanistic to say that the way in which the Community has evolved reflects among other things the underlying logic of the purposes for which it was created and of the institutional means which were chosen for achieving them. It is particularly important for a British audience that we should be clear about this logic – which is often not very well understood on this side of the Channel – not only because it helps to explain why the Community is as it is, but also because it illuminates the limits within which we can hope to change it.

The Europe in which the Community came into being after the last war was divided into a set of distinct national economies, each subject to a large degree of national government control and each separated from the other by differences between the ways in which the government's control was exercised. The fundamental purpose of the Community's founders was of course to promote European political unity. However, the removal of the economic barriers between the European states and their replacement, where appropriate, with instruments for control by the Community was also held to be an important purpose in its own right. For while the achievement of European economic unity removes one of the basic obstacles to political union and helps people to learn to work together as Europeans, it also has the effect of promoting the more rational development of the European economy as a whole.

The essence of the Community system as it has worked up to date can thus be summed up in a sentence, as the removal of artificial economic barriers between the member states, and the replacement of national economic regulations, where appropriate, by Community policy; this economic strategy being a means to a wider end – that of closer European political union.

This system first took shape in the construction of the European Coal and Steel Community (ECSC) in the early 1950s. After the war, in spite of the way in which Europe's coal and iron fields straddled frontiers, its coal and steel industries presented a vivid example of the fragmentation of the European economy. Each was subject to close regulation by the different national governments, pent up within their national boundaries.[1] The only way to achieve a single market for coal and steel was to remove these different structures of governmental regulation of the national markets; but because of economic and social conditions in the industries, and because of the politics of German recovery, this could not be done simply by abolishing all regulation – Community instruments were required to replace the national ones. Accordingly a supra-national High Authority for the ECSC was created, counter-balanced by a Council of national Ministers and an indirectly elected parliamentary assembly. To this new Coal and Steel Community were transferred national powers to regulate investment, production and subsidy; and national measures which might have the effect of disrupting the unity of the market were banned.

The experience of the ECSC was a success; but this was not the only reason why the institutional structure which it pioneered was adopted five years later when it was decided to tackle the even more ambitious objectives of establishing a European Common

---

1. The German industries were still, of course, under Allied control, but this was being wound up. One of the basic political purposes of the ECSC was to provide a European alternative to the return of strategic industries to German national control.

Market and customs union, and an atomic energy Community. For in both cases the problems were the same as that with which the ECSC began: the segmentation of the European market by distinct national policies which it was impossible simply to abolish but which had, within limits, to be replaced by a single Community policy.

The creation of a Common Market and customs union entailed three main consequences in addition to the straightforward removal of tariff and non-tariff barriers to trade. Competitive conditions between the national economies had to be equalized where different national policies might create inequalities – that is to say there had, most fundamentally, to be an equalization of the burdens of agricultural support[2] and, in due course, a harmonization of economic and monetary policies. Further, there had to be a unified commercial – and to some extent, therefore, a unified economic – policy towards the rest of the world. And because the creation of the Common Market would disrupt many long-settled patterns of production, not only in agriculture but also in industry, Community policies had to be developed for cushioning the processes of change and helping adjustments to take place.

Clearly measures as far-reaching as these required not merely *the co-ordination of distinct national policies* but also the creation of a set of institutional and political arrangements capable of defining a *common policy for the whole of the Community*. Because it was set up to deal with fundamentally similar problems, and had done so successfully, the Coal and Steel Community provided an appropriate model; and, accordingly, institutions similar to those of the ECSC were established in 1958 for the new European Economic Community ('Common Market') and European Atomic Energy Community ('Euratom') – the three organizations being merged into a single European Community (EC) in 1967.

The Community's history in the 1960s was essentially that of the

---

2. This is why, in the late 1950s, the British government was unable to conclude a free trade area agreement with the Community, by which Britain could have the benefit of tariff-free access to the Community market for her industrial products without sharing in the cost of supporting continental agriculture. Such an arrangement could be as impossible to negotiate in the 1980s as it was in the 1950s.

working-out of the logic of the original decisions embodied in the founding Treaties. In this first phase, which lasted roughly between 1958 and 1969, the main themes were the removal of barriers to intra-Community trade, the establishment of the Common Commercial Policy and the policy for overseas development, and the negotiation of that inevitable counterpart of industrial free trade and the customs union – the Common Agricultural Policy.

At the end of the 1960s, however, a second phase began, through which the Community is still passing. This phase has been marked, on the one hand by the effort to maintain the achievements of the 1960s and to continue the working-out of the logic of the Treaties, and on the other by attempts to go beyond the immediate objectives of the Treaties to the achievement of further and deeper measures of economic, monetary and political integration. To this second phase there belong the Community's drive to harmonize national economic management policies and achieve monetary union, and its efforts at 'political co-operation' – that is, the harmonization of foreign policies.

The Community's evolution in its first quarter-century has, therefore, had two main features: the fulfilment of the objectives originally laid down in the Treaties; and the development of a new and wider range of tasks. The present distribution of functions within the Community and the pattern of growth from which it has arisen is illustrated in Figure A (see page 33). This shows how the Community is organized around a central core of areas of policy reserved for decision-making through the institutions set up by the Treaties (circle 1). This central core has been expanded into new areas (circle 2). And around this there have also emerged additional subjects of decision-making through organs of the Community not established in the Treaties (circle 3). The Community's historical development has roughly speaking moved outwards from the central core through the development of the concentric circles indicated in the figure. Its future course will be largely shaped by the transfer of functions from one circle to another – for example, so the authors hope, the further transfer of activities from exclusive member state competence (circle 4) to 'co-operation', and from 'co-operation' to the 'central core'. And the direction and pace of these developments will in turn be set by our experience of the relative capacity – or incapacity – of these different modes of decision-making to meet Europe's needs.

Figure A: The Community's Functions

1. Decision-making by the Treaty institutions on subjects specified in the Treaties. For example the removal of barriers to trade and the free movement of persons, services and capital within the Community, the Common Agricultural Policy, the Common External Trade Policy, the Community's Overseas Aid Policy, the Social Fund, and aspects of policy for coal, steel and nuclear energy. Note that decisions in relation to some of these subjects are specifically reserved by the Treaties for unanimous agreement in the Council of Ministers. The rest are intended to be decided by a majority vote, qualified or simple, weighted according to a formula most recently defined when Britain, Ireland and Denmark joined the Community in 1972.

2. *Functions added to this 'central core'*, either under the evolutive Article 235 of the EEC Treaty (see p. 73 below) or by the resolutions and declarations of 'Summits' and Council meetings: for example, under Article 235, the Community's Regional Policy, its policies for the environment and for consumer affairs, certain financial powers and powers in the energy sector.

3. *'Co-operation'*, whether on a Treaty basis and through the Treaty institutions, or on the basis of intergovernmental agreements and through organs of the Com-

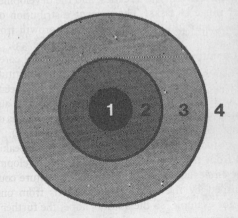

munity not established in the Treaties. An example of the first type is the system for managing the convergence of the economic policies of the member states; of the second is the system of 'political co-operation' or diplomatic concertation which has developed since 1970 within the 'Conference of Foreign Ministers' and its subordinate structures linking the Foreign Ministries of the Member States.

4. *Member state functions.* This includes functions over which decisions are made mainly or exclusively by the member states – for instance, most of education, health and social services. And also functions which are the subject of co-operative international decision-making within a non-Community framework – for instance, defence. Here it is interesting to reflect on the large range of subjects over which experience shows that exclusively national decisions are by themselves increasingly inadequate.

An important point which Figure A cannot illustrate is the relative significance of the functions falling within the various circles. These cannot all be measured on the same scale: it is not possible, for example, to weigh the significance of the Community's Common Commercial Policy alongside that of – say – the as yet uncoordinated expenditure of the member states on unemployment benefits. Nevertheless a financial comparison is effective if crude. In itself the Community's budget is quite significant, and it has been growing fast – in 1979 it will amount to some £8,630 millions, equivalent to some 12 per cent of forecast British public expenditure, and it will have grown by more than 600 per cent over the previous ten years. But the most striking thing a comparison shows is that while public expenditure in the member states in 1975 was about 45 per cent of the gross product of the Community as a whole, direct expenditure by all the Community institutions was no more than 0·7 per cent. These figures should be compared with the 20–25 per cent of the gross product which is spent by the federal authorities in the United States and West Germany: they show how very long is the Community's road ahead.[3]

3. MacDougall, Report on the *Role of Public Finance in European Integration*, April 1977, Vol. I, pp. 12–13, published by the European Commission at Brussels. Note, however, that these figures do not take account of the Community's indirect expenditure which is undertaken by the member states when they implement Community policies – a large part of the national customs and agricultural administrations, for instance, are, in practice, acting as agents for the Community.

The Institutions[4]

Within the area of Community decision-making based on the Treaties (circles 1 and 2) the Community's system of government is marked by two fundamental characteristics. First, it operates according to a 'written constitution' – the Treaties – of which the European Court of Justice is the final interpreter. Second, it is a system based on a concept of the balanced integration of national and supra-national authorities.

The Court of Justice consists of nine judges appointed for six years by agreement among the member state governments. It settles disputes by applying Community law at the instigation of the Commission, or of a member state or of individuals or enterprises affected by Community legislation. It also gives 'interlocutory' judgements at the request of national courts seeking the authoritative interpretation of the Treaties and of the 'derived Community law' which flows from them.

One effect of these arrangements is to provide for the uniformity and the primacy of the Community's system of law in all the member states. Another is to ensure its autonomy. In the Community – as, for instance, in the United States – the Treaty/constitution embodies a public policy standing over and above the will of governments; and the Court is capable of playing a dynamic and creative role by way of the interpretation of that policy.

The other principle underlying the Community's government – that of the balanced integration of national and supra-national authorities – is reflected in the character and membership of the Community's basic institutions and in the distribution of roles and powers between them. These matters are the subject of the whole of this study. Here the point being made is that each of the Com-

4. This account – and indeed the whole of this chapter – is intended primarily as a constitutional analysis of the functioning of the Community. An excellent but rather different account – perhaps it is a little too sobering – has been written from a political-behavioural point of view by Helen and William Wallace and Carole Webb (eds.), *Policy Making in the European Communities*, John Wiley, London, 1977.

munity institutions has both a national and a supra-national aspect, and that these two aspects are so closely interrelated that they cannot be separated one from the other: indeed the national and the European levels in the Community's institutional structure are so interrelated that they form a single constitutional system which is neither national nor supra-national but which is in effect a new form of trans-national political association.

The Court is supra-national in the sense that its judgements are final. Its members are, however, nominated by the national governments. Its basic texts are at one and the same time both constitutional law and international law. Similarly, the Commission's thirteen members have a supra-national role – symbolized, for instance, in their oath of independence at the beginning of each four-year period in office. But, like the Court, the Commission is also nominated by the national governments – although, as with the Court, the nominations must be made in agreement. And while it has limited executive powers of its own, its most important functions can only be carried out in conjunction with the Council of Ministers: thus again illustrating the interdependence of national and supra-national authority in the Community.

For the Council, too, is both national and supra-national – supra-national in its role as the Community's legislature, national in its composition and in the executive responsibilities of its members.

Only a directly elected EP might be regarded as being an essentially supra-national institution with its members drawing their mandate direct from the European electorate as a whole – even if, for the time being, this mandate is given through different national electoral systems. Indeed, this way of looking at the EP has led some people – both supporters and opponents of direct elections – to argue that the Parliament might act as a sort of constituent assembly for a united Europe, taking it upon itself to widen the functions of the Community beyond those agreed by the member states in the Treaties.[5] All that needs to be said of this view at this

5. For instance, in February 1976 Willy Brandt made a speech arguing that 'the EP must be the "voice of Europe". It has the opportunity and the obligation to give more definite shape to the European identity and to create those powers which a European government needs in areas of common responsibility. It will therefore

stage is that it is hardly realistic. The legitimacy of a directly elected EP will derive from the Treaties as well as from election. And while, as this study shows, there is a great deal of room for interpretation, the Community's constitution both circumscribes the powers of the EP and lays down the procedures by which they may be increased – procedures in which national authority has a pre-eminent place.

Making and Administering Community Policy

Within the framework of these institution, how is the Community's policy formed, and how are decisions made and put into effect? Here we have to pay regard not only to the Community's formal constitutional structure but also – and perhaps even more – to the way in which it actually works in practice. Figure B (pp. 38 and 39) summarizes the Community's decision-making process.

Four stages of policy-making may be distinguished:

1. Initiation.
2. Formulation.
3. Adoption.
4. Execution and supervision.

The Initiation of Policy

In constitutional form the Treaties confer upon the Commission the exclusive power to draw up proposals for action by the Community in almost all the areas of policy reserved for Community decision (circles 1 and 2 in Figure A). Within this area the Commission determines the timing of the initiation of proposals, it

---

have to see itself as the permanent constituent assembly of Europe'. Subsequently Michel Debré followed up the argument from the opposite point of view, asking 'is it to be thought that an assembly elected by direct universal suffrage, its own master when it comes to deciding the length of its sessions, its agendas and its procedural rules, and at liberty to create all the committees it wants and to grant its members a privileged status, [that such an assembly] will respect the limits that have been set on its powers?'

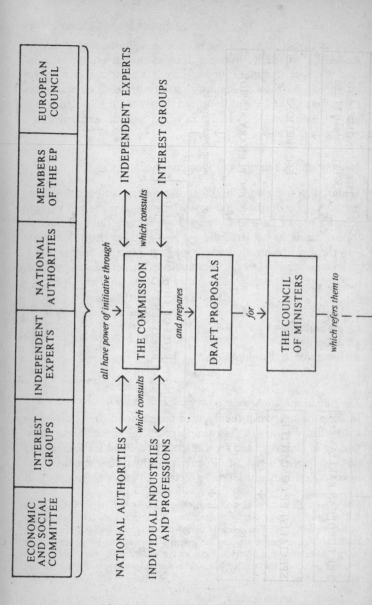

ECONOMIC AND SOCIAL COMMITTEE	INTEREST GROUPS	INDEPENDENT EXPERTS	NATIONAL AUTHORITIES	MEMBERS OF THE EP	EUROPEAN COUNCIL

all have power of initiative through

NATIONAL AUTHORITIES ← which consults → INDEPENDENT EXPERTS

INDIVIDUAL INDUSTRIES AND PROFESSIONS ← which consults → INTEREST GROUPS

THE COMMISSION

and prepares

DRAFT PROPOSALS

for

THE COUNCIL OF MINISTERS

which refers them to

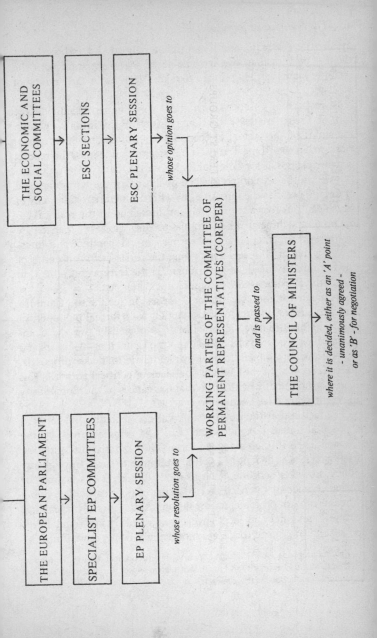

THE EUROPEAN PARLIAMENT → SPECIALIST EP COMMITTEES → EP PLENARY SESSION

whose resolution goes to

THE ECONOMIC AND SOCIAL COMMITTEES → ESC SECTIONS → ESC PLENARY SESSION

whose opinion goes to

WORKING PARTIES OF THE COMMITTEE OF PERMANENT REPRESENTATIVES (COREPER)

and is passed to

THE COUNCIL OF MINISTERS

where it is decided, either as an 'A' point
- unanimously agreed -
or as 'B' - for negotiation

must write the texts, and it can unilaterally amend and withdraw them – powers that give it some scope for negotiation with the member states as they prepare to take a decision in the Council of Ministers.

In respect of co-operation (circle 3 in Figure A) outside the core of Treaty matters, the Commission has the initiative within the ambit of the system of economic co-ordination which is provided for in the Rome Treaty. It initiates the guidelines, the reports and any proposals for Community legislation that may be required. But within the area of 'political co-operation' or the harmonization of foreign policies the initiative lies with the member states, any of which can put forward proposals for discussion in the political co-operation machinery. The Commission does, however, participate in these arrangements and it can play an independent and intermediary role at all levels – including the thrice-yearly meetings of the Community heads of government in the European Council, in which the President of the Commission takes part.[6]

So much for the constitutional forms. In reality the Commission's role is less impressive. Although it has a formal monopoly of the right of initiative, in practice it is obviously not the Community's only source of policies; and the Council of Ministers and the European Council frequently 'invite' it to make proposals. Indeed, because of the Commission's lack of political authority this is in fact how many of the important advances of the Community in recent years have been made.

The fact is that the Commission will not generally put forward a proposal unless it stands some chance of being accepted by the Council, even if in an amended form. The Commission cannot by itself generate sufficient of a political impulse to carry through any policy, however sensible or far-sighted. Rather, it has to wait for the emergence of the necessary coalition of political forces, doing what it can to promote its evolution. And generally speaking, although regional and local governments and national and European-scale pressure groups are increasingly being drawn into the

6. The European Council is thus a 'hybrid' institution operating at the highest level both of the Community's Council of Ministers and of the system of 'political operation' outside the Treaty framework.

Community's activities, the political forces that have to be brought into line are those embodied in the national governments.

A classic instance of both the scope and the limitations of the Commission's role in policy-making is afforded by the current proposals for a 'European Monetary System'. Since 1973 the Community's progress towards economic and monetary union had been suspended, basically because of the absence of a sufficiently extensive and powerful consensus among the member governments about both the objective and the next steps. However, at the end of 1977, his first year as President of the Commission, Mr Roy Jenkins staked his personal credibility and that of the Commission on a re-suscitation of the project of economic and monetary union; and his persuasive efforts and the technical groundwork done in the Commission certainly made an important intellectual contribution to the emergence in the course of 1978 of a renewed coalition in favour of the project. But the decisive factors were the political changes in France after the National Assembly elections in March, which gave President Giscard a freer hand to pursue his European policies, and the reaction of the German government to the continuing slide of the dollar and the relative appreciation of the Deutschemark. With the re-emergence of a Franco-German coalition in favour of a European Monetary System the necessary political conditions for reopening the question were established; and the way was opened for the Commission to advance specific proposals for putting into effect the broad lines of policy approved by the heads of government at the European Council at Bremen in July 1978.

What effect will direct elections have on the ways in which the political coalitions which are necessary for Community initiatives emerge and take shape? So far, the essential political forces amongst which a degree of consensus has to show itself are those embodied in the national governments. But governments are not monolithic entities, and they are themselves subject both to internal and to external pressures. What success the Commission has had up till now in stimulating the emergence of the degree of interest necessary for its proposals to be given serious consideration has depended largely upon its ability to exploit the internal divisions within governments – for example those between Foreign Office and Treasury, or central bank and Ministry of Finance, or President and Prime Minister – and to play upon such external pressures as the fall in the value of the dollar. One of the most important political functions of the new European Parliament will be to magnify the effect of such divisions and pressures and to widen the arena within which the Community's political processes work themselves out. A directly elected Parliament will of course help to form a more highly developed public opinion about Community affairs: most important of all, it will increase the involvement in them of the political parties from among which the national governments are drawn.

The Formulation of Policy

Under the Community's constitutional arrangements most draft texts prepared by the Commission are submitted to the European Parliament and the Economic and Social Committee (ESC) so that they can give their opinion before the Council decides. As we shall see, the Parliament normally proposes whatever changes it wishes to make in the form of detailed amendments to the Commission's text. We shall discuss in Chapter 3 the way in which this process of consultation works, along with the EP's various budgetary and legislative processes.

In the field of economic co-operation the EP and the ESC are, naturally, consulted about proposals for legislation, and they are also associated with the annual cycle of reporting and discussion of economic policy issues. In 'political co-operation', on the other hand, the nine member states act not by promulgating detailed legislation but by passing resolutions and making declarations to whose formulation the European Parliament makes no direct contribution: although, as we shall see, it is able to hold debates and ask questions about policy in this field.

In political reality, however, the formulation of Community policy is as much subject to the necessities of consensus-building as is its initiation, which we discussed in the previous section. The chief function of the Parliament in this respect is that of bringing under review, public scrutiny and debate the rationale and implications of the Commission's proposals and the objections to them. Up till now, however, the Parliament's discussions have not received much public attention. After direct elections this should change, so that the Parliament's opinions acquire more weight in the Community's political process from the enhanced public interest lying behind them.

The Adoption of Policy

If, within the Treaty framework, the initiation and formulation of Community decisions by the Commission, the EP and ESC represents the drafting stage of legislation, the work of legislation proper is in effect done in the Council of Ministers – or, to be more practical about it, in the working groups of officials meeting in the Council framework.

There is an interesting contrast between decision-making in the Community and in the member states. The formulative stages in the Community are relatively very much more open, but the making of the final decisions is much less so. The Council deliberates behind closed doors: in practice it is as much a forum for inter-governmental negotiations between the member state bureaucracies as a legislative body.

Nevertheless, the Council *is* a legislature. It acts by passing,

i. *regulations*, which apply directly as law in the member states;
ii. *directives*, which bind the member states as to 'the result to be achieved', but not as to the means;
iii. *decisions*, *recommendations* and *opinions*.

To this list might also be added a fourth category of non-Treaty Acts – *resolutions* and *declarations* which have political but not legal force, and which it is important should not become substitute for Community legislation proper.

In spite of its character as the Community's legislature the Council's procedures for decision-making are highly bureaucratic. Its study of the proposals and opinions which have been submitted to it is mainly carried out in a network of committees and working parties made up of officials from the member states and the Commission. The penultimate stage in this process is reached in the regular weekly meetings of the nine Ambassadors – or Permanent

Representatives – which prepare the meetings of the Council. The COREPER, as this official committee is called (after its acronym in French), has acquired a virtual legislative power of its own by informal delegation from the Council.

However, the final decision in most important matters is made after discussion in the Council of Ministers itself. The 'general' Council consists of the Foreign Ministers of the member states with Commissioners in attendance, but the Council also meets in a variety of 'special' forms – whether, for instance, as agriculture ministers discussing agriculture, or as finance ministers considering financial questions.

The Treaties provide that the Council of Ministers' decisions be made by a majority vote, qualified or simple, unless unanimity is expressly required. The vote is 'weighted' to give the four larger countries ten votes each, Belgium and the Netherlands five each, Ireland and Denmark three each, and Luxembourg two. Out of this total of fifty-eight votes, forty-one constitutes a majority. An important safeguard for smaller countries, and for the Commission's right of initiative, is that, while the Commission's proposals may be adopted by a majority, they can only be amended unanimously. The Parliament also benefits from this provision when – as we shall see it frequently does – the Commission decides to adopt as its own an amendment made by the Parliament to its original text.

In spite of these provisions, majority voting in the Council is still in practice exceptional – save in budgetary matters. The Treaties themselves restrict its employment; and although they envisaged its wider use after 1966, this was blocked by de Gaulle, who argued that essential national interests could not be overridden by majority votes. This position was accepted by the other member states in the so-called 'Luxembourg Compromise'. However, at the 'Summit' of December 1974 France took the lead in reopening the door – at least part of the way – and a certain number of decisions has since been made by show-of-hands or on a basis of abstentions, including, for example, the decision in 1977 to establish the Community's JET thermonuclear power experiment at Culham in Oxfordshire. The question of what constitutes an essential national interest nevertheless still remains to be defined; or rather, perhaps, the member states are still not yet confident that we have reached a stage of integration at which the proper functioning of the Community's institutions will ensure that the vital interests of one are regarded as the vital interest of all.

In what sense are the European Council, the Council of Ministers and the COREPER democratically accountable? Until now this question has not pressed because the practice of deciding unanimously in the Council has preserved the theoretical accountability of the national ministers through their national parliaments to their electorates at home: in theory any national parliament can require its government to veto a measure, thus blocking the Council as a whole.

However, in practice, even when decisions are made by unanimity, this system of accountability is unsatisfactory for at least two reasons. First, the accountability asserted in this way can only be negative. Because it controls only its own national ministers no national parliament can bind the Council as a body to some positive achievement; its power can only be that of stopping, not of starting. Second, in any case in practice the national governments quite reasonably refuse to have their negotiating positions in the Council restricted by their parliaments. To accept such restrictions would hamper them in their pursuit of the national interests with which they are charged; and it is also recognized that it would be impossible to make any Community decisions at all if every Council act had to be confirmed by the national legislatures before it could take effect.

Under the qualified majority rule laid down in the Treaty this 'accountability gap' will become even wider, since voting in any form denies even the theoretical possibility of national parliaments controlling the Council through the national power of veto. The implications of this situation for the European Parliament are discussed in Chapter 6 below.

The Execution and Supervision of Policy

Community policies are implemented in three ways:

i. by the Commission exercising independent power of authorization and supervision given it by the Treaties, or powers of implementation granted to it by the Council – for example in the coal, steel and nuclear sectors, in trade policy, in respect of the Common Agricultural Policy, the Social, Regional and (overseas) Development Funds, Community research, the competition policy, the customs union, and in the authorization of waivers of Community rules ('derogations') when special circumstances require it;

ii. by the Council – although not organized as such, the Council in practice often acts like an executive, given the detailed nature of many of the decision it takes;

iii. by the member states acting as the Community's agents in the implementation of directives and the administration of the customs union, of the Common Agricultural Policy and of the various Community Funds.

The Commission has an important role in the implementation of the Community policy as the guardian of the Treaties, seeing to it that the member states carry out their obligations. As for its own role as an executive, it has executive powers over an impressive range of subjects, but its activities are in fact closely controlled by the member states. Each Community Fund has an attached committee of government representatives, as does the administration of most of the common policies. Some of these committees are purely consultative. Others – for instance, the 'management committees' which have been set up in connection with agricultural market-management and the customs union – have a quasi-executive role, for if the officials representing the governments do not agree with the Commission's proposal, the Commission can go ahead but has to give the Council a chance to overturn its decision.

As we shall see in Chapter 3 the Commission's decisions are subject to a measure of formal accountability to the EP. However, the EP has rather less control over the Council and none over the representatives of the member states; and neither, in practice, do the national parliaments. Here again we meet with the problem of the 'accountability gap'.

Nevertheless, while parliamentary control in the Community is gravely defective, legal and financial control is relatively highly developed. The Court of Justice has an important role to play in ensuring the full and correct application of Community law, both by the Commission and the Council and by the member states. And in respect of financial control there has now come into operation a European Court of Auditors consisting of nine members appointed by the Council in consultation with the EP.

The Originality of the Community System

What sort of a system is the Community? From the point of view of constitutional theory it might perhaps be best described as a species of confederation in which, as the British Foreign Minister, Dr David Owen, recently expressed it, 'sovereign states cede to a central authority the responsibility for handling certain common matters, while retaining a measure of control on common business, and undisputed authority over everything for which responsibility has not been transferred to the centre'. The key point – to which perhaps Dr Owen's definition does not give sufficient emphasis – is that the system is a dynamic one in which the area of 'common business' is expanding and in which, alongside the central core of common matters, there is growing up an increasingly institutionalized practice of co-operation in the exercise of powers still formally retained by the member states.

The Community's essential institutional dynamic in the 1970s has lain in the way in which, as this system of co-operation has become more intense in economic matters and foreign policy, the distinction between the operations of the 'central authority' and the 'sovereign states' has become increasingly blurred, and procedures which were at first without binding significance have tended to become regularized and formal. Over the years ahead we can expect this process to continue; and it is also probable that there will be periods of consolidation and rationalization when informal conventions that have hardened are made over into formal institutions, and what was originally in principle voluntary is formally recognized as obligatory. Thus the range of operations of the Community will expand – as it is now doing in the sphere of economic and monetary management – and at the same time the obligations (and the opportunities) of membership will become increasingly powerful.

At the beginning of this chapter we saw how the purposes for which the Community was created imposed their own logic on its institutional structure – in particular by making it necessary that there should be some element of supra-nationality in the Community's constitution. On the other hand, we have also seen how, in the Community's political process, the member state governments have kept the upper hand in deciding and executing Community policies, if not also in initiating them. Yet the preponderance of the national governments in the Community system is increasingly affected by the entry into the arena in which Community policy is made of an expanding range of political forces – regional and local governments inside the Community, foreign governments and lobbies abroad, and political parties and pressure groups operating not only on the national but also at the European level. This is a system which defies attempts to describe it in simple terms. But perhaps analogy is instructive. As one distinguished commentator has pointed out, there are many 'parallels to be drawn from the disjointed and dispersed power structure of American politics: an established and effective federation, but one in which the distribution of power between levels of government and the continuing commitment of federal politicians to state and district interests makes for a structure far more complicated than any blueprint for "union" could ever have envisaged'.[7]

7. William Wallace in H. and W. Wallace and C. Webb, op. cit., p. 313. In his discussion of the work of some of the early American theorists of European integration, Mr Wallace emphasizes the parallel: 'one cannot but be amazed that American political scientists, familiar as they were with the political deadlocks, the log-rolling, the awkward and irrational compromises and the concern for parochial constituency interests which characterize the multi-level system of American politics, should nevertheless have theorized about a developing United States of Europe which would miraculously display none of these basic political characteristics'. See p. 302.

Meanwhile, however much the member state governments may have been able to keep the reins of decision in their hands, the fact is that the Community continues to develop as something rather more than an association of sovereign states joined together for strictly defined and limited purposes, like the OECD and NATO and all the other international and inter-governmental organizations in which the industrialized democracies participate. The originality of the Community system remains, along with the potential for its future development.

In sum, there are five original features of the Community system.

First, the legal framework provided by the Treaties is qualitatively different from that embodied in the looser statutes of the traditional inter-governmental organizations. It has power to make laws which are directly applicable to individuals in the member states. 'Over a significant field of Community activity the rule of law has been established, with the authority of the European Court of Justice sufficient to adjudicate in case of doubt and to command the compliance of companies and government.'[8]

Second, the Commission has a very much more powerful role and status than the secretariats of other multinational organizations. It has achieved a degree of political authority which enables it to play a leading part in defining the issues for Community debate – as Roy Jenkins has done in connection with the revival of economic and monetary union. And it has significant powers of management in particular sectors such as agriculture, the Common Commercial Policy and the overseas development policy.

Third, Community politics are very much more publicly visible than are those of the classical inter-governmental organizations. Community issues are the stuff of national headlines. 'The European Communities may not yet have established themselves as a focus for popular loyalty transcending the nation state; but they *have* clearly established themselves as a focus for popular attention, as an accepted element in the domestic political debate in all the member states'.

8. This and the citations which follow are from W. Wallace, op. cit., pp. 318–20.

Fourth, as we shall see further in the next chapter, the Community possesses its own financial resources, drawn from sources of funds directly under its own control. 'If politics within nation states revolve around the resolution of conflict and the distribution of rewards, then the establishment of a Community budget – however small and however overbalanced by the Common Agricultural Policy it may be – represents a move towards the creation of a recognizable political system at the Community level.'

Finally, and from the point of view of this book the most important feature of all, the Community will shortly be the only multinational organization endowed with a directly elected Parliament. It is thus 'a political system in the process of formation [rather] than an inert inter-governmental framework'. Over the decades ahead direct elections occurring one after the other every five years will help to fix a pattern of rising popular awareness and expectations; and their regular recurrence is almost a guarantee of the Community's permanence and its capacity for future development. Unless a catastrophe intervenes, there will be European elections in the summer of the year 2029: what will Europe be like then, fifty years hence?

Chapter 3: The European Parliament's Powers and Functions

A fundamental distinction that should be observed in the discussion of all political arrangements is that between the *formal* and the *real* – a distinction which is related to that set out in the title of this chapter, between *powers* and *functions*. The importance of these distinctions lies in the fact that the formal distribution of constitutional powers – the abstract, legal–theoretical framework of a constitution – may be very different from the realities of the political structure as it works in real life.

Understanding of this difference between the formal–theoretical and the informal–real should come easily to a British audience, because it is in fact one of the fundamental principles of British constitutional development. With us it is a matter of pride that by changing the realities while keeping the same forms we have been able in the past to secure both greater political stability than our more doctrinaire neighbours, and a form of government that fits satisfactorily the changing needs of the times. Examples in British constitutional history are legion, one of the most striking of course being the role of the Monarchy – in constitutional form still keeping all the powers and prerogatives prescribed by the late-seventeenth-century settlement, but in practice exercising only a vestigial influence in politics.

The 'Westminster Model'

From the point of view of this study, however, the most interesting British example of this distinction between the formal and the real is that of the House of Commons, for the gap between theory and practice at Westminster sheds an illuminating light on the powers, functions and procedures of the European Parliament.

Subject to the residual constitutional powers of the House of Lords and the Crown there is no doubt at Westminster about the constitutional primacy of the House of Commons. The continuance in office of Her Majesty's Government depends upon its votes, the day-to-day conduct of government business is subject to a wide-ranging power of scrutiny, and no legislative act can be made without its consent. It is, however, notorious – as it were by application of the paradox of British constitutional development, separating form from reality – that the role in practice of the House of Commons is in no way commensurate with its formal powers.

Although the classic distinction between the legislative, executive and judicial powers was formulated after the settlement of the British Constitution in the seventeenth century, it can be usefully applied to it. In this analysis the British executive lies in the Queen's Ministers and permanent officials; and the question that must be asked in assessing the effective powers of decision of the House of Commons is, how much real control do its back-bench Members and the opposition parties have over the life and acts of the executive in the shape of the Queen's Government? The answer is, of course, that in the normal circumstances of a government with a working majority they have very little control, and that even in the recent exceptional case of minority governments, their power is not much greater.

The explanation lies in the way in which the 'executive' in Britain has come to dominate the House of Commons through the development of the party system and the government's power to dissolve parliament. Ordinary members may in theory vote the government out at will: in practice the majority of them are normally subordinate to the government whip. Members may in theory at any time throw out the government's legislative proposals or amend them almost without limit: in practice the same whip brings them into conformity with government policy, even in the most trivial matters. Members may in theory ask any questions and set up any inquiry they choose (although because of the fiction of ministerial responsibility they may not press Whitehall too hard): in practice, again, the discipline of sustaining the government curbs tongues and sees to it that even the best-argued criticisms of policy, commanding wide assent among the back-benches on both sides of the House, are given no effect if the government finds it inexpedient.[1]

The House of Commons, then, is a striking example of the distinction between the formal and the real: in a phrase, it possesses the forms without the substance of power. On the other hand, this is not to say that the House of Commons lacks all *influence*. It plays a crucial role in forming and informing public opinion. More than any other institution it defines the 'atmosphere' in which government must be carried on. And, above all, it sets the context in which political careers are made and broken.

But this influence is not based on the House of Commons' formal powers which have, in fact, been captured by the executive. There is probably a psychological connection between the Commons' formal powers and its influence. But the House gets its prestige not so much from its constitutional potentialities as from historical tradition and from the functions it fulfils in our politics – notably by virtue of its monopoly of recruitment to high ministerial positions. Its influence in politics is consequently indirect, based on its role as the 'forum of the nation'; it is not a direct result of the exercise of effective decision-making powers.

A number of conclusions relevant to the future of the EP can be drawn from our analysis of the situation at Westminster.

Of these the most interesting is the paradox that too much formal power may have the effect of constraining a parliament's real powers of decision. Thus the main reason why governments in Britain have taken control of the House of Commons is that, according to our constitutional doctrine, they must do so in order to survive. Since, by a perhaps unwarranted application of the theory of parliamentary supremacy, every negative vote can be

1. Looking for signs of the rise of back-bench influence is one of the favourite sports of most political commentators, and the period of minority government since 1976 has provided some notable examples. But this period must still be regarded as the exception rather than the rule; and in any case the most notable feature of the period since 1976 has surely been, not the uncontrollability of the House of Commons under minority government, but the ease with which in general the government has been able to carry on its business and retain the initiative by manipulating the various blocs into which the opposition is divided.

construed as touching the life of the government, clearly the 'executive' cannot afford to relinquish any of the practical instruments by which it holds parliament in thrall.

Similarly, the illusion of constitutional power may inhibit a parliament in seeking to expand its real influence as a forum for persuading and informing – as an institution where debates mould as well as express public opinion. The weaknesses of the House of Commons in this respect arise in part because the 'executive' fears not only adverse votes but also adverse criticism and the exposure of inconvenient facts – so that party solidarity constrains not only voting behaviour but also the expression of opinion. But this disinclination on the part of the government to surrender any portion of its power is also reinforced by the attitude of those parliamentarians – whether careerists or romantics – who prefer the shadow of power to the substance of influence. For up till now the debates about procedural reform in the House of Commons have been dominated by those who would rather have powers they cannot use than reforms that might require a lessening of those theoretical powers, but which would confer the possibility of expanding the real influence of the House.

The European Parliament, by contrast, can have no illusions about its constitutional powers, which are minimal compared with those of the House of Commons. It will of course use what powers it has to the full and seek prudently to increase them – *some* powers are indeed necessary as a fulcrum on which certain kinds of influence may be made to turn. But the EP should never lose sight of the fact that its objective is influence, rather than the acquisition of formal marks of respect. And in this respect, as we shall see in the present chapter and the next, the mixture of powers, procedures and functions with which the new Parliament will start its life offers quite sufficient scope for a role of increasing influence.

The powers and functions of parliaments in general may be described under five headings:

(1) participation in the appointment and dismissal of the executive;
(2) scrutiny and control;

(3) legislation;

(4) the recruitment of political leadership;

(5) representation, communication and the mobilization of opinion.

It is against the background of this analysis of parliamentary functions in general that we will seek to describe the role of the EP, to assess the significance of its powers, and to indicate some of the possibilities for their further development.

Participation in Appointing and Dismissing the Executive

As we have seen, in the Community executive power is divided between the Commission, the Council of Ministers and the member states.

The EP cannot of course participate in the nomination of the Council. This is a function for the separate internal constitutional processes of the member states. It follows that while the EP may pass any sort of resolution on a matter falling within the sphere of the Community, it cannot hope to affect the composition of the Council by expressing a lack of confidence in its decisions.

In this respect its relation to the Council regarded as the Community's executive is analogous more to the relationship between the United States Congress and the American executive than it is to that between the House of Commons (in theory) and the 'executive' in Britain.[2] In particular the EP will sit for a fixed term of five years, and the Community's executive will lack the power of dissolution which is – together with the party system – the basis of the government's control of the House of Commons. For its part, because the EP lacks the powers of appointment and dismissal in relation to the Council it must find other ways of exerting a measure of influence over the executive role in the Community of the Council and the representatives of the member states; and

2. In Britain the 'executive' sits in the legislature. In the Community, on the other hand, a formal incompatibility has been agreed between membership of the European Parliament and membership of the Commission or the Council of Ministers.

in this, as we shall see below, it can draw upon the experience of Congress and in particular of its committee system. In so far as it is felt that the possession of formal powers over the composition of the executive may give it greater practical influence, the Parliament might press for the transfer of executive functions now performed by the Council and its subordinate bodies to the Commission – over whose appointment and dismissal it may hope to increase its constitutional power.

For if the EP does not and cannot have any say in the nomination of the Council, the Treaties already give it powers in respect of the dismissal of the Commission, if not of its appointment.

Under the Treaty the EP may require the Commission to resign as a body by passing a motion of censure by a two-thirds majority of the votes cast, provided that this amounts to a majority of all Members. Whether this power of dismissal could be turned, in practice, into a power to approve appointment – by the Parliament deciding to 'veto' all appointments that do not meet with its approval – would depend essentially upon the political climate in which such a confrontation between the EP and the member state governments were to take place. Probably the EP would be well-advised to avoid such a confrontation; but that is not to say that it cannot hope to achieve a growing influence over the appointment of the Commission, as recommended by the then Belgian Prime Minister, Mr Leo Tindemans, in his report in 1975 on European Union.[3]

If and as the EP's influence in the appointment of the Commission increases, the question will arise as to whether the Parliament should attempt to impose any particular political balance upon the Commission. It is of course unlikely that any political Group would be able to muster the necessary two-thirds majority in Parliament to achieve its purpose by threatening to dismiss any Commission

3. Mr Tindemans' proposal is that the EP should have the power to approve the nomination of the Commission's President and his programme. He should then himself have a right to approve the nomination of his colleagues. Perhaps some sort of 'confirmation' procedure on American lines might be introduced, if not for all the Members of the Commission at least for the President. This would certainly be less radical than Mr Tindemans' implied proposal that the EP should have the right to approve not only a man but also a programme.

not of its preferred political hue. But quite apart from this practical consideration, it must be asked whether the Community will or should evolve in such a way that the Parliament might impose an exclusive political colouring upon the Commission. This suggestion is commonly associated with the idea that the Commission should evolve into a European government; and that the European constitution should be based on a parliamentary system. However, in the loose quasi-federal Community system that exists at present and will continue for the foreseeable future, two things are clear: that the master institution in the Community is the Council, which will continue to be a fluctuating coalition of different political tendencies; and that the essential role of the Commission will continue to be the working-out of technically sound policies and the effort to mobilize a wide consensus for their implementation. The imposition by the Parliament of an exclusive political complexion upon the Commission would not touch the heart of the Community's coalition system in the Council; and it would certainly reduce both the technical competence of the Commission and its ability to promote a consensus for its policies.

The same considerations should also be borne in mind when we consider the suggestion that the EP should acquire – perhaps by threatening to dismiss the whole Commission – the power to dismiss individual Commissioners. Short of the ancient and disused power of impeachment, parliaments do not normally enjoy the power to dismiss individual Ministers: because of the doctrine of collective responsibility, any such vote is normally regarded in most political systems as a vote of no-confidence in the executive as a whole, requiring its resignation as a body. On the other hand, under the procedures already established, there is nothing to stop the EP from passing a motion of censure on any individual Commissioner, just as the House of Commons may do so by way of a motion to reduce a particular Minister's salary.[4] And the political effect of such a vote of individual censure might be enough to

4. The EP, incidentally, would have to find some other formula than this, since, as we shall see below, Commissioner's salaries are part of the Community's 'obligatory' expenditure and are therefore not subject to the requisite degree of parliamentary control.

induce the Commissioner concerned to resign even though he would be under no obligation to do so. But would the negative effects of the development of such a procedure upon the Commission not outweigh the possible benefits? Collective responsibility and collegiality are, after all, doctrines that have evolved for a good reason; and although the Commission is not an executive in the same sense as is the government of one of the member states, it too can plead the advantages of coherence, stability and independent judgement that flow from the principle of collective responsibility.[5]

The Scrutiny and Control of the Executive

The powers of scrutiny and control generally enjoyed by parliaments consist of two instruments both of which the EP in some measure possesses. These instruments are:
(a) the right to ask questions – both written and oral – and to call the executive to account in public plenary session and in public or private committee debates;
(b) prospective and retrospective control of the budget.

Questions and Debates
In respect of the first of these instruments the Treaties give the EP the power to adopt its own rules of procedure. But they differentiate between the rights it has over the Commission, which is obliged to reply to its questions, and its rights over the Council – which decides for itself the conditions under which it 'shall be heard' by the EP.

A series of decisions by the Council and agreements with the EP over the years now ensures that a Council representative – as a

5. It could, on the other hand, be argued that precisely because the Commission is not a 'government' it has less need than governments do of collective responsibility, and that the advantages of asserting the Commission's dependence upon the Parliament would outweigh the disadvantages of weakening the Commission. To the extent that the Commission itself might accept this argument, thus refusing to resign as a body in the event of the censure of one of its Members, it may be that the EP could have a more effective power of censure over individual Commissioners than do most national Parliaments over national Ministers.

general rule its President or one of its Members – takes part in the EP's plenary sessions and in meetings of its committees. As we shall see in the next chapter, on the Parliament's procedures, a 'Question Time' has developed at which members of the Commission and a representative of the Council Presidency answer oral questions at each of the plenary sessions. And the Conference of Foreign Ministers has made the same arrangements in respect of debates and questions concerned with 'political co-operation' matters outside the Treaty framework.

There is, however, still room for greater openness on the Council's part to questions and debates in the EP. With the exception of the President of the finance ministers Council dealing with budgetary matters, the Presidents of 'special' Councils do not take part regularly in the EP's plenary sessions; and neither does the head of government presiding over the European Council. More fundamentally, while the Council legislates behind closed doors it is questionable whether its proceedings can be subjected to adequate public debate when it is represented before the EP only in the person of its President: at present the Parliament has no official way of learning the positions taken up by the different national delegations – and very often those positions are not disclosed in the national parliaments either, on the argument that secrecy suits the national interest in 'international' negotiations.[6] This is an interesting example of the 'accountability gap' which we discussed

6. This issue, and the problems it will raise after direct elections, was the subject of an interesting statement by the President of the EP, M. Georges Spénale, in November 1976, when the President-in-Office of the Council made an evasive reply to an oral question. 'President – Ladies and Gentlemen, I should like to tell the President-in-Office of the Council, and I feel I am speaking for the whole House, how much importance we attach to this last question addressed to the Council. It is absolutely essential that the Council should think again about this problem, since the replies which have been given are not satisfactory.

'In fact, after replying "we cannot speak about these matters because they are confidential", you add "but you can ask your Minister for the answer in your national Parliament". In other words, the President-in-Office of the Council can reply in the Netherlands Parliament, as the Netherlands Minister for Foreign-Affairs, to those of our colleagues who are Members of the Netherlands Parliament, but he cannot reply to them here as President-in-Office of the Council. This means that from the Council, which is a Community institution, we can only obtain

in the previous chapter: probably it will only be bridged eventually by recognizing that the Council is in essence a legislative body – a sort of upper House – which should deliberate in public. But at this stage in the Community's evolution, with the Council fulfilling roles which are both executive and legislative, it is still necessary for efficient decision-making that the Council should normally work in secret. So long as this is so, however, there will be a case for building on the experience of the 'Conciliation Committees' (see p. 72 below) to give the EP the right to question all of its Members together, not just its President – thus complementing the powers of the national Parliaments over national Ministers and reinforcing parliamentary control.

The development of the EP's relations with the Council is of course intimately bound up with that of its legislative functions, which is discussed on pp. 68–74 below. Meanwhile, the main task facing the directly elected EP in the matter of questions both to the Council and to the Commission will be to exploit the full potential of the powers it already possesses. These, and its existing facilities, are already considerable. It is not so much the acquisition of new powers of question and debate that will make an impact, but the fact of doubling the size of the EP and equipping it with full-time Members directly responsible to a Europe-wide electorate and better able than the present Members to make full use of their opportunities.

For it is clear that whatever influence the Parliament may be able to build up in the Community's political process will depend – at least at first – more upon the merits of its arguments and upon its capacity to bring public opinion into focus than upon its formal

---

fragmentary replies in our national parliaments! Furthermore, by a curious prismatic process, the replies which our Ministers give to our national parliaments do not always coincide exactly, which is not satisfactory either. When we have a Parliament elected by direct universal suffrage where the dual mandate will not be obligatory, it will become really intolerable if only members of national parliaments are entitled to a reply on Community questions while Members of the European Parliament are not. It is a problem which must be thought about and to which a solution must be found, failing which we shall have conflicts.' Debates of the *European Parliament*, No. 289, November 1976, p. 87.

powers to hold the Commission or the Council to account. In this respect once again the appropriate model is the United States Congress, whose influence in the processes of American government depends not only upon the power to say 'yea' or 'nay' to the proposals of the executive but also upon its ability to argue with it and expose its weaknesses in its positions.

Here the directly elected EP will begin its work with an important asset in the shape of the Committee system which has been developed over the past twenty years (see pp. 93 ff.).

The main growth in the EP's activities immediately after direct elections is likely to be in this area, where the Parliament's effectiveness depends not so much on the acquisition of new powers as upon its own decisions – for instance, as to whether Committee debates and 'hearings' should be held in public or not – and upon the co-operativeness of the Commission and the Council.

Budgetary Control

The history of parliaments shows that their original power – from which their legislative powers derive – lies in their monopoly of the right to supply taxes. In modern circumstances, however, the power to control expenditure is perhaps more important than the power to tax. Hence it is significant that the most developed of the EP's present powers are to be found in the sphere of Community expenditure.

The EP's powers over expenditure are of two types, *prospective* and *retrospective* – that is to say powers to approve expenditure before it is made, and powers to check whether expenditure has been properly made.

Retrospective budgetary powers. Ex post facto control of expenditure is not, of course, a check on policy but a check on administration. However, it is an important dimension of parliamentary responsibility for the budget, and it represents a powerful instrument of investigation and accountability.

After receiving an opinion from the Council the EP is now the sole institution giving a financial discharge to the Commission – the formal closing of the books on a financial year. The EP is assisted in this task by the newly created Audit Court, which will have an independent power of investigation of the use made of Community funds, and which will be able to make public statements attaching blame and making suggestions for avoiding future mismanagement. The EP's relations with the Audit Court – an independent body – are a politically delicate issue; but the Court will be able to draw particular issues to the Parliament's attention, make reports and provide the necessary expert opinions.

Inside Parliament a control sub-committee of the Budgets Committee has existed for the past three years. This is a tentative step towards a public Accounts Committee. Already the sub-committee has shown its teeth in obtaining confidential documents from the Commission and in reviewing the efficiency of expenditure as well as its formal regularity.[7]

Prospective budgetary powers. Underlying the Community budget, and justifying the powers exercised by the EP over it, is the principle that the Community is financed by its 'own resources'. Originally the Community's activities were paid for essentially by separate national contributions fixed according to an agreed scale. But since 1971, after the parliaments of the member states had given their assent, the 'own resources' system of automatic Community revenues has been coming into effect.

By this system, which will be complete by 1980, the Community receives directly, in its own right and without the intervention of the national parliaments, all revenues from levies on agricultural imports, all customs duties and the proceeds of a rate of value-added tax up to 1 per cent, levied on a common assessment base. To illustrate the sizes of these three factors, the financing of the draft budget for 1979 is estimated to be met by £1,350 millions

7. 'Following direct elections, Parliament's sub-committee, which could usefully be transformed into a full committee, should, working closely with the Court, be able to cut down frauds and abuses in the agricultural sector. Although in the past the Commission has sometimes been reluctant to transmit to Parliament "confidential" documents relating to expenditure, it will become increasingly difficult for the Commission to refuse to hand over internal documents when so requested by Parliament.' Michael Palmer, 'The Role of a Directly-Elected European Parliament', *The World Today*, XXXIII (1977), pp. 122–30, on p. 125.

(15·4 per cent) from agricultural levies, £2,989 millions (34·2 per cent) from customs duties, and £4,290 millions from a rate of VAT of 0·75 per cent (49·1 per cent of the total Community revenue).

Subject to a 'financial mechanism' which partially links net national transfers into the Community budget to the national share of the Community's gross product, after only twenty years in existence the Community thus disposes of its own independent revenues. The powers of the EP over Community spending are, however, subject to two major restrictions.

First, the 'own resources' are inelastic. The agricultural import levies and the customs duties are fixed by the Community, but the decisions are not made with an eye to their revenue-raising implications. And any decision to increase the Community's share of VAT revenues above 1 per cent or to give it new resources, thereby increasing its overall expenditure powers, can only be made with the agreement of the national parliaments. Second, there is a difference between the EP's powers over the Community's so-called 'compulsory' or 'obligatory' expenditure and its powers over 'non-obligatory' expenditure.

The distinction between the two types of Community spending is based on the fact that certain expenditures arise directly and automatically from the Treaties and from the legal acts implementing them – and these are therefore 'compulsory' or 'obligatory'; while other expenditures arise from decisions which broaden the range of Community activities and are therefore not obligatory under the Treaties. The EP's powers to approve expenditure are stronger in the latter, smaller, sector.[8]

8. 'A parallel can be drawn between the limitations on the European Parliament's power to amend the compulsory provisions of the budget, and the limitations which exist on the rights of Members of Parliament in budgetary matters in four of the member states. In France, Members can reduce or abolish items of expenditure, but can only increase them if alternative provisions are made elsewhere; in Italy, Members can propose increases and reductions in taxes and expenditure, but cannot create a new item of taxation or expenditure; in the United Kingdom, Members cannot increase expenditure or taxation without the permission of the Government, but can reduce expenditure and taxation, and in Ireland, Members cannot move amendments to the budget. The European Parliament's position in

In relation to 'obligatory' expenditure the EP has the right merely to be consulted – but, by the principle of the so-called 'inverted majority', if the Council does not rejects those of the EP's proposed amendments which do not lead to a net increase in expenditure, they stand. The EP also has the power to reject the whole of the budget, including its 'obligatory' elements.

In relation to 'non-obligatory' expenditure a Treaty amendment in 1971 gave the EP the last word, provided that it can satisfy certain stiff requirements concerning majorities. Thus the EP has the right to amend the Council's draft budget at first reading by a majority of its Members; and if the Council modifies these amendments, the Parliament can prevail at the second reading, acting by a majority of its Members and three-fifths of the votes cast. These procedures, and the practical working of the Community's budgetary process, are further discussed on pp. 105–8.

The point to note about them is that experience so far tends to show that it is not so much the EP's rather limited powers of overruling the Council which are an effective source of influence, as the opportunities to shape policy which arise from the many 'collaboration' meetings that take place between Parliament and Council during each budgetary cycle.

The EP's powers over 'non-obligatory' spending are, moreover, subject to a further constraint, additional to these provisions for a qualified majority and the overall inelasticity of the Community's revenues. The Budget Treaty provides that there shall be a 'maximum rate' at which non-compulsory expenditure can be increased. This maximum rate is calculated annually by the Commission on the basis of objective economic factors – the trend of the gross product of the Community, the increase in national budgets and in the cost of living. It defines each year a certain range within which the annual growth of the Community's 'non-obligatory'

---

budgetary matters vis-à-vis the Council of Ministers is, then, similar to that of M Ps in the member states vis-à-vis their governments.'

Valentine Herman and Juliet Lodge, *The European Parliament and the European Community*, Macmillan, London, 1978, pp. 37–8. It might further be pointed out, however, that – as we shall see below – the EP has the power to vote *increases* in expenditure.

expenditure must be confined. The power to increase spending within this range is shared between the Council – acting on the Commission's proposals – and the EP. If the Council's plans for increasing the Community budget take up less than half of the amount allowed under the maximum rate, the EP is entitled to claim the remainder; and if the Council's proposals exceed half that amount, the EP is automatically entitled to a further half. In addition, the Council and the EP may decide jointly to fix a new maximum rate. Indeed in practice, while the rate calculated by the Commission acts as a dampener on expenditure increases, the EP and the Council have so far negotiated a new rate at the end of the budget procedure. In this way in 1977 the EP added £113 millions or 1·3 per cent of the total to the budget.

How might the EP's budgetary powers be further developed?

Here we must make a distinction – to which we will revert in our discussion below of the legislative functions of the EP – between the 'vertical' increase of powers and their 'horizontal' expansion. The EP's powers are increased 'vertically' when it is given additional legal powers; its influence expands 'horizontally' as the range of operation of the EP's existing legal powers expands with the growth of the Community's activities.

Since in the 'non-obligatory' sector the EP already has the last word, the key to any 'vertical' increase in this sector must be the acquisition by the Community and the EP of more extensive powers over taxation than those implied in the Community's existing revenues. Only then can the EP complete its control of 'non-obligatory' expenditure by increasing or abolishing the 'maximum rate' of annual increase; and only then can the EP's budgetary powers be expanded beyond its present powers of expenditure control.

The present arrangements in fact point in this direction. For one thing, as we have seen, the Community's budgetary system gives the EP the right not only to approve but also to initiate considerable and increasing expenditures – spending for the 'supply' of which it has only a very limited responsibility. The only way in which this anomaly can be put right is by giving the EP the more visible powers over taxation without which such responsibility cannot be exercised.

Moreover the revenues available to the Community will reach their ceiling in the not too distant future – perhaps by 1981 – when the 1 per cent share of VAT is fully taken up. The 'enlargement' of the Community to include Greece, Portugal and Spain will necessitate an increase in the budget without any change in the existing policies. And, apart from any progress now being made towards economic and monetary union, enlargement will certainly increase the pressure for the expansion and improvement of the machinery for effecting 'resource transfers' through the Community budget. These factors, together with the growing criticisms now being made of the regressive character of the Community's revenue system – bearing most heavily upon the poorer countries and the poorer consumers – indicate that during the life of the first directly elected Parliament there will have to be a major overhaul of the Community's finances. One of the most important tasks of the new Parliament will be to see to it that it grasps this opportunity to try to achieve a 'vertical' increase in its powers both over expenditure and over taxation.

Passing from the 'vertical' to the 'horizontal' expansion of the EP's budgetary powers, the basic point to be remarked is that the area covered by the budgetary powers of the EP tends naturally to expand as the amount of the Community's 'non-obligatory' expenditure increases each year within the maximum permitted rate. In a sense it grows too as the EP improves its budgetary procedures and secures improvements in the presentation of the budgetary aspects of Community decision-making. And it is also likely to expand as and if the argument about the precise boundaries between 'obligatory' and 'non-obligatory' expenditure moves in favour of a directly elected EP.

For although the classification of expenditure under these two heads is a legal rather than a political matter, in practice the precise location of the boundary is open to a degree of interpretation in which the Parliament has had considerable success in its efforts to persuade the Council.

In 1971, the first year of the operation of the new budgetary system, the Council classified only 3·6 per cent of the Community's total expenditure as 'non-obligatory' – some £60 millions; but by 1977 the boundaries had shifted and the proportion had risen to 19 per cent or £1,186 millions. And in 1977 the argument about the status of the Regional Fund was resolved in favour of the EP's view. Moreover a number of important areas of dispute remain – for instance the classification of expenditure like that under the Agricultural Guidance Fund, which is 'compulsory' as a whole but which can be sub-divided into non-compulsory elements, and the classification of spending which arises from international agreements made by the Community – for instance the Community's fund for disaster relief.

The ultimate 'horizontal' expansion of the EP's budgetary powers would be, of course, the extension to the 'obligatory' sector of the powers which the EP at present enjoys over 'non-obligatory' spending. This would, for instance, bring the funds provided for agricultural intervention-buying within the EP's control, thus giving it a decisive voice in the development of the Common Agricultural Policy. It might be objected, however, that such an expansion of the EP's powers would bring to completion a fundamental transformation in the nature of the Community which is still only in its early days. At the root of the distinction between the two types of expenditure and the degree of control to which they are subject is the concept of the Community as a creature of inter-state agreement embodied in the Treaties. By the removal of that distinction the Community would finally have established itself as an autonomous political entity with an existence of its own above and beyond the will of the member states. For the time being this would not perhaps be regarded as an acceptable development, least of all in Britain: but the day will surely come when it is regarded as a reasonable price to pay for the imposition of a measure of real parliamentary control over the agricultural policy.

Meanwhile the autonomous status of the Community is already implied in the EP's power to reject the whole of the Community budget *in toto*, in the existence of the 'non-obligatory' sector of the budget, in the powers of the EP over it and in the practice of majority voting in the Council on budgetary matters. But these are still no more than pathways into the future; they are neither a stopping place nor the destination itself.

Legislation

The law-making powers of parliaments in general can be variously categorized, reflecting subtle nuances of power and influence which may range from the mere right to express an opinion to a decisive power to bind the executive to the will of the legislature. It is also normal for parliaments to have greater powers over some areas and certain types of legislation than over others. The EP exhibits both of these features: the possession of a manifold of types of powers over legislation, and a variation in their incidence. The chief difference between the EP and most of the national parliaments is that it lacks that upper range of power positively to bind the executive that the latter enjoy in theory and – in varying degrees – in practice. On the other hand, the European Parliament has the compensating advantage, at least as compared with Westminster, that it can play an active part in the pre-legislative stages of Community law-making.

A different scheme of powers over legislation could be described in every parliament. The analysis in this chapter is based on the following ascending hierarchy of powers, with all of which except the last two – 3(b) and (c) – the EP is in some measure and in certain areas endowed.

1. The power to pass resolutions:
    (a) no obligation upon the Council to consider them;
    (b) The Council obliged to consider them.
2. Consultative powers:
    (a) consultation at the discretion of the Commission and the Council;
    (b) in the event of consultation, no obligation upon the Council to give an explanation if it rejects the EP's opinion;
    (c) the right of the EP to an explanation.
3. Legislative powers proper:

(a) the power of delay;

(b) the power of veto;

(c) the power to make positive resolutions requiring action.

The Power to Pass Resolutions

The power to pass resolutions is one of the bases of the power of parliaments. It is one of the chief instruments by which parliaments carry out their duty to represent, and it is the root of the power to initiate legislation.

The Treaties give the EP a full measure of power to pass resolutions. Indeed in this respect the EP is master in its own house to a far greater extent than is the legislature in the Westminster model of government – in which, as we have seen, the theoretical dominance of the legislative over the executive power has led to the practical dominance of the latter over the former. The EP decides for itself the timing of its sessions, their duration, its agenda and its rules of procedure, and the resolutions which it may or may not entertain; while in the House of Commons all of these matters except the last – the voting on which will normally be decided by the whips – is in the hands of the government.

The EP does not, however, possess the formal power to initiate Community legislation: as we saw in Chapter 2 this is a power which is reserved to the Commission. There is nothing, however, to prevent the EP casting some of its resolutions in the form of draft Community legislative texts which might then be adopted and put forward by the Commission.[9] This possibility is further considered on p. 142.

Within the present arrangements, however, there is no obligation upon the Commission either to act upon the EP's resolutions or to adopt its legislative initiatives; nor is the Council formally obliged to consider the Parliament's 'own initiative' resolutions or to give any explanation for rejecting its opinions. Here again, though, the Parliament's lack of formal rights and powers does not necessarily mean that its resolutions or any draft legislative texts it

9. Similarly at Westminster the best hope for a Private Member sponsoring a bill is to have it taken over by the government or debated in government time: otherwise the power of back-benchers to initiate legislation is essentially a fiction.

may adopt are without influence. They may – and after direct elections they certainly will – have a considerable political impact, particularly since the Commission's power of initiative, unlike the EP's power to pass resolutions, is confined to the field prescribed for it by the Treaties.

By contrast, if the EP were to be given a formal right – perhaps initially by convention – to have its resolutions considered by the Council, as proposed in Tindemans' report, it would not only be able to get the Council's response to its views on subjects not raised by the Commission, but it would also be able to put on the agenda of the European Council, if not of the Council itself, proposals going beyond the scope of the Treaties. This would give the elected representatives of the European people as a whole their appropriate share in decisions about the pace and character of the advance to European Union which have up till now been reserved for the heads of government of the member states. It would also constitute a significant step forward to a power of legislative initiative.

Consultative Powers

The Treaties provide for the obligatory consultation of the EP on proposals for legislation on a wide range of subjects. In addition the Council has extended the range of consultation to subjects on which it is not obligatory.[10] The Commission has declared itself willing whenever possible formally to amend its proposals so as to embody the EP's amendments in its proposals, and the Council has also agreed that the EP should normally be reconsulted if substantial amendments are made in Council to proposals upon which the EP has already given its views. The Commission must

10. One of the most important developments in this respect is in the field of external relations. Consultation here is a delicate business because external relations issues usually involve negotiations with third countries, and they may involve 'mixed' procedures – a mix of Community and member state agreements. The EP may therefore need to be informed rapidly and confidentially. This occurs through the so-called 'Luns-Westerterp procedure': Parliamentary Committees are informed by the Commission of the progress of negotiations and the President of the Council informs them of the content of an agreement when it is initialled but before it is concluded by the Council.

obviously now see to it that the EP is always given enough time to form an opinion before final decisions are made.

The distinction between discretionary and obligatory consultation of the EP has thus in practice been largely abandoned. The important question at this stage in the evolution of the EP's consultative powers is rather that of the Council's response to their exercise. This is bound up with the further issue of the Council's willingness to answer the EP's questions and participate in its debates. Apart from the arrangements which have been made for this, and which were discussed on p. 59 above, it has been agreed that the EP's President may inquire in any particular case why the Council has chosen to depart substantially from a position taken up by the EP. The next step in the development of the EP's consultative function would be to require the Council, like the Commission, to give its reasons on every occasion that it fails to follow the Parliament's view.[11]

Legislative Powers Proper

The power of delay. In 1975, after the Community's 'own resources' financing system – see p. 62 above – had begun to come into operation the EP, the Council and the Commission made a 'Joint Declaration' according the EP the germ of a power of suspensory veto over decisions 'of general application' which give rise to 'important expenditure or revenues to be charged or credited to the budget'.

Although its opinion is not binding on either the Council or the EP, it is the Commission's responsibility to determine when these conditions apply. This Declaration in effect acknowledges the

11. Cf. Commissioner George Thomson's statement to the Parliament in December 1976 concerning its legislative work in 1975 and 1976: 'During this period of two years, Parliament has given 281 opinions on the Commission's proposals. The vast majority of these – 207 – have been favourable ones. In 74 of its reports Parliament has proposed amendments, and in 52 out of these 74 cases the Commission has been able to accept them either partly or wholly. In only 22 cases has the Commission been unable to follow Parliament's amendments. Moreover, during the course of the debates on these 22 issues Parliament has very often shown that it appreciated the Commisssion's reasons for being unable to follow Parliament's advice.'

logical connection that exists between budgetary and legislative powers, that control over a budget cannot be effective without a measure of control over the legislation giving rise to it.

The procedure is that when the Council is proposing to depart substantially from the EP's opinion, and the Council and the EP agree that the other conditions are satisfied, a Conciliation Committee is set up consisting of the Council – all its Members – representatives of the Commission, and a delegation from the EP. If this Committee decides that the Council and the Parliament are in a position to reach agreement, the proposal is re-submitted to the Parliament, which delivers a second opinion on it. Agreement must be reached within three months, failing which the Council is free to proceed; and if a decision is urgent the Council may fix a shorter time-limit.[12]

The legislative power accorded to the EP is thus minimal: it consists of the elements of a suspensory veto – for three months – and of a right to negotiate with the Council. But experience to date, especially in relation to the Financial Regulation implementing the budget, is that it significantly expands the Parliament's opportunity to exercise its influence. And while the status of the 'Joint Declaration' is no more than that of a gentleman's agreement, its very informality holds out the possibility of its more extensive use and, indeed, its expansion in due course. The logic of the interdependence between budgetary and legislative powers is not yet exhausted; and as the former widen and develop, so the latter must follow in their train.

The power of veto. But will the appetite of a directly elected EP for a real measure of influence over Community law-making be satisfied by these arrangements for a minimal suspensory veto, and will

12. 'Concertation procedures' similar to these exist in a number of the parliaments of the member states. They are used in France, Germany and Ireland to reach agreement between the two Chambers of the legislature. In France, Italy and Germany the executive has a power like that of the Council in relation to the EP to request the legislature to reconsider a law. And in a number of member states the executive also has the 'last word' – a right to refuse assent – to legislation. V. Herman and J. Lodge, op. cit., p. 33.

it be prepared to wait for the link between legislative and budgetary powers to continue to work in its favour?

In 1972 the Vedel Report on the *Enlargement of the Powers of the European Parliament*[13] argued that while the EP's legislative powers should not be permitted to develop so as to replace those of the Council – that is to say it should not acquire the ultimate legislative power to make positive resolutions requiring action – its consultative role should be developed into a real power of co-decision with the Council, based on an ability either to delay or to accept or reject Council decisions. The implications of such a development for the national parliaments are discussed on pp. 147–50. Here we will confine ourselves to summarizing Vedel's proposals as indicating the direction in which the EP might develop if it were decided to enlarge its powers over legislation.

Vedel proposes that these powers should be enlarged in two stages. During the first stage the EP should be given powers of veto ('co-decision') over a limited range of subjects, and powers of delay ('suspensory veto') over a wider range. In the second stage its suspensive powers over the latter class of subjects should be raised to a power of co-decision.

The subjects over which a power of co-decision should be accorded in the first stage, 'materially involve either the Community's constitutive power or its relations with other persons in international law'. These include the revision of the Treaties, the implementation of the evolutive article 235 of the Rome Treaty,[14] the admission of new members, and the ratification of international agreements concluded by the Community. It should be pointed out in connection with this list of subjects that it is obviously appropriate that a directly elected EP should play a leading role in any formal affirmation of the Community's commitment to

13. Vedel Report, Brussels, 1972, pp. 37–49.
14. 'If action by the Community should prove necessary to attain, in the course of the operation of the common market, one of the objectives of the Community, and this Treaty has not provided the necessary powers, the Council shall, acting unanimously on a proposal from the Commission and after consulting the Assembly (the EP) take the appropriate measures.'

democracy that may be made in the context of the accession of Greece, Portugal and Spain.

The subjects over which Vedel proposes a power of suspensory veto in the first stage, to be subsequently raised to a power of co-decision, are concerned with (i) measures for the harmonization of legislation, and (ii) questions of principle affecting the common policies which might give rise to harmonization measures. Harmonization is one of the Community's basic legislative activities, and it is also one of the most controversial. It might be hoped that those national parliaments which are most anxious to ensure that such measures are more fully debated will be the first to welcome the EP's acquisition of a power to delay or prevent their introduction.

On the question how far the development of these legislative powers would require a revision of the Treaties, Vedel argues that while it is desirable that any enlargement of the EP's powers be firmly anchored in amendments to the Treaties, in fact only the grant of a power of 'co-decision' would necessitate such a revision.[15] This judgement would seem to be confirmed by the 'Joint Declaration' which has subsequently granted the EP the limited powers of suspensory veto of which we have already given an account.

The Recruitment of Political Leadership

So far our discussion has focused on the EP's powers in the constitutional sense – its powers to dismiss the Commission, to hold the Commission and the Council to account, to vote the Community budget and to share in the Community's legislative process. This section and the next concentrate mainly on the Parliament's functions in the Community's political processes; and they take up under a different aspect the basic distinction we drew at the beginning of this chapter, between formal powers and real influence.

One of the most important political functions of parliaments generally is to supply a recruiting and testing-ground for political leadership. However, the extent to which the legislature supplies

15. Vedel Report, pp. 82–5.

the personnel of the executive varies widely in Western democracies, from the American and French Presidential systems at one end of the scale – where the executive is recruited mainly from outside the legislature – to the virtual 'closed shop' which has evolved at Westminster for members of the British parliament aspiring to ministerial office.

Political leadership is, moreover, not a function whose exercise is reserved exclusively to parliamentarians and ministers. Where the system of government is decentralized, as in the United States, Germany and – increasingly – in Britain, there are to be found important regional and local political leaders who are recruited through 'lower tier' representative institutions. In all modern societies the leaders of the great organized interests – trade unions, big companies – have acquired a wider political role which is not based on any parliament. And the increasing scale and complexity of government today has given policy-making officials in the public service a political function which defies any attempt to distinguish sharply between elected and non-elected political leadership.

The EP's role in recruiting political leadership must be set against this complicated background. There is no doubt that the position of its members in this matter will be more like that of French *députés* or members of the United States Congress than that of members of the British parliament. Under the present arrangements there is no ladder of promotion into the executive to which they have a monopoly – or even a privileged – access. On the other hand it is probable that the career-patterns of members of the directly elected EP will be very much more variegated than those of British MPs; and it is possible that the EP will supply recruits to a rather wider range of positions of political leadership – at regional, national and European levels, in the private sector and in the public service – than is the case at Westminster.

Will the Commission come to be drawn from the ranks of the European parliamentarians? We have already discussed the EP's power to dismiss the Commission and the proposal that it should share in the nomination of its President. It is possible that these powers might evolve towards a form of privileged access for members of the EP to membership of the Commission. But in the foreseeable future it would not be desirable to risk damaging the connections between the Commission and the member states from which Commissioners are drawn; and in the longer run it remains to be determined whether the best form of government for the Community is a parliamentary regime.

With regard to recruitment to the Council, European parliamentarians can only hope to enter it by using their membership of the EP as a base for entering the political processes by which the executive is recruited at the national level.

The EP itself will of course tend to develop its own internal career structure, as has happened in the United States Congress. The greater the EP's influence, the more sought-after will be its Committee Chairmanships, its Presidency, etc.

But perhaps the most important role that the EP will play in the recruitment of political leadership in the Community will be that of supplying a new dimension of politics. It should open the way to political careers which are acted out in a variety of forums – parliamentary, ministerial, in the great interest groups and in the public service; and on a series of different levels – European, national and regional. In most continental countries service in the EP will not be regarded as a career by itself, but will take its place as one possible step in a path which already leads quite naturally back and forth between the national and regional levels. There is a danger that in Britain, by contrast, the lesser flexibility of the political system will lead to careers at Westminster and in Europe being regarded as alternative choices for life. If this is so the calibre of British members of the EP will probably turn out to be relatively poor; and the House of Commons and ultimately, therefore, the quality of the British government's contribution in the Council will also be the poorer.

Communication, Representation and the Mobilization of Opinion

Among political scientists nowadays it is generally agreed that the constitutional powers of modern parliaments in the making of policy are less significant than their wider political functions in mediating between government and the governed.[16] This is essentially the conclusion we reached in our discussion of the role of the House of Commons at the beginning of the chapter. What is important in a parliament is its capacity to act as a focus for the aspirations of the electorate, as a forum for the articulation of their grievances and hopes, as a place of debate where conflicting interests and values are resolved, and as an intermediary between the executive and the people – transmitting impulses from one to the other and serving in particular to rally public opinion behind the policies of the government.

Certainly it is true that in each of the Western democracies the trend since the palmy days of the parliamentary system in the mid nineteenth century has been for the executive to gain an increasing dominance over the law-making functions of the legislature. And, as we remarked earlier, nowhere has this trend been more pronounced than at Westminster.

However, it cannot even be affirmed that parliaments have been adequately compensated in their wider political role for their loss of real influence over legislation. The emergence of mass political parties, together with the growth of the influence of organized interest groups outside parliament and the development of the modern technologies of mass communication, have led to parliaments being more and more by-passed even in their role as intermediary between government and governed. Additional – and even alternative – channels of political communication continue to emerge: for example the referendum, and 'corporatistic' tripartite discussions between the executive and organized labour and capital. And the dominance of the executive – provided that it can secure the support of the great interests organized outside parliament – continues to grow.

In short today the position of representative parliamentary institutions in general, both in the systems of government of the democracies and in their political processes, is weak and probably growing weaker. This has important implications – to which we shall return

16. This is, for instance, the opinion of most of the galaxy of authorities writing in *European Integration and the Future of Parliaments in Europe*, published by the European Parliament, Luxembourg, October 1975.

at the end of the last chapter – for the relationship between the national parliaments of the Community and the directly elected EP.

Viewed against this sombre backdrop of the declining influence and significance of parliaments in general, what are we to make of the EP's *political* – as opposed to its strictly *constitutional* – potential?

Here it seems to us that the EP is in a relatively strong position. Its present role, both constitutional and political, is one of little influence. But for reasons that are further discussed in the last chapter, a directly elected EP is in a position to make an essential contribution to the development of the Community – a contribution which it alone can make and which therefore gives it the chance to play a vitally important part in that development.

Historically, it might be argued that the basis of the influence of parliaments in the last century lay in their contribution to the integration of the nation state – whether the integration of classes in Britain, or the integration of ethnic groups in America, or that of regions as in France. At the national level this role has now perhaps been largely played out, and new political structures are emerging in which parliaments figure less prominently. But the work of European integration, by contrast, is still only in its early days. The EP must look to make the same kind of contribution to European integration as the national parliaments have made to the integration of the national states.

It will do this in the same way as they have done, by acting as a focus of communication and as an instrument for representation and the mobilization of public opinion.

First, *communication*. Just as the contribution of the parliaments to national integration could not have been made without the newspaper press in its classic age, so the EP's contribution to European integration must take full advantage of television and radio – which have already shown themselves capable of building audiences on a continental scale. At the national level television and radio have diminished the role of parliaments in political communication, in some measure because the parliaments have been unwilling to adapt. The EP must not make this mistake. Its members must have the best possible facilities for access to the media; and both at its plenary sessions and at 'hearings' – public meetings of its Committees with outside participants – its procedures should be designed with that purpose largely in mind. The Commission and the Council could assist in this by developing the practice of making policy announcements at the EP's plenary sessions.

Above all the EP must realize its strategic advantage as the only publicly accessible European institution. The Council deliberates in secret, and in any case it can be presented in public terms only as a focus of national activity. The Commission also works behind closed doors and its members are bound by their collective responsibility. By contrast, the EP exists to dramatize European issues, to debate them and demonstrate their relevance and immediacy. As a focus for European political communication it will be unique: for it television will not be a rival but an ally.

Second, *representation*. The main political function of parliaments has always been to supply a channel through which organized opinion can be represented in the process of government – thereby influencing it, and, in return, being brought to accept its authority. How will this work in the case of the EP?

In the Community today opinion is still organized almost exclusively at the national level, where it is organized either around political parties or around economic and social interests. Initially at least, the politics of the EP will inevitably be a projection of these forms of national political organization, and the first test of the Parliament's integrative power will be its capacity effectively to represent these forces and engage them in the European political process. Here it starts with the great advantage that it is the only European body in which the opposition parties as such are represented.

Party politics in the Community are fully discussed below in Chapter 5. Here we will confine ourselves to a discussion of the EP's role as a focus for the representation and mobilization of opinion in the widest sense. In respect of the political parties the essential point is that the present indirectly elected EP has succeeded in avoiding the establishment of separate national delegations and has evolved a party structure which is essentially trans-national in character. At the same time the effectiveness of its Committee system ensures that debate does not degenerate into sterile inter-party confrontations, and it gives the political forces an opportunity to influence Community legislation in a reasoned way.

Outside the EP, the prospect of direct elections has also stimulated the development of trans-national alignments between political parties. The Christian Democrats and the Liberals have both formed integrated European parties which will put up candidates on a single platform in several member states. The Socialists are drawing up a common programme; and the Conservatives are co-operating increasingly closely with the Christian Democrats. These developments are already having significant effects on party organization and leadership both outside and inside – with the consequence that the EP is becoming an increasingly important focus of party political activity.

There remains, however, something of a question-mark over the relationship between the EP and the economic and social interest groups which now exercise such great influence at the national level. It should, however, be noted that the EP's position in this matter is relatively stronger than that of the national parliaments. Interest and pressure group activity at the Community level is still relatively under-developed – except perhaps in the agricultural sector – and it is difficult to organize and make effective. For some time at least, the EP will be well placed to act as an essential channel of communication between the Community's executive and organized public opinion – especially if the EP takes care to foster a mutually helpful relationship with the Economic and Social Committee.

Meanwhile, as the Community's political system evolves a life of its own – and as the political life of the member states continues to develop, for example towards greater regionalism – is it not probable that forms of political organization will emerge at the European level which are not simply the projection of the existing national political forces?

One aspect of this will probably be the increasing autonomy of the European political parties. But perhaps in the long run of even greater significance may be the emergence of a European pattern of politics closer to that of the United States – a pattern of politics in which party plays a rather less important but still essential role. The Community's implicit constitutional structure is closer to that of the United States than it is to that of any of the member states, except perhaps France; and it seems that the separation of the executive from the legislative power makes for a political system in which parties are relatively weak and politics is organized around *ad hoc* coalitions of interest and opinion. Issues like devolution to the regions, environmental policy, nuclear energy and European integration already cut across orthodox party – and national – boundaries in the Community. And as the scope of the Community's activities and expenditure increases a parallel may emerge with American 'pork barrel' politics, in which legislators act more as the representatives of local areas, regions and interests than as the bearers of a coherent party ideology.

The EP's internal procedures – which are, of course, entirely under its own control – will be a significant factor in determining the pattern of its politics. Two topics in particular stand out: petitions and 'hearings'.

The development of national representative institutions owes much to the right to petition the executive through parliament. Nowadays in Britain this procedure has largely fallen into disuse – although in a sense it has evolved into the practice of writing letters to MPs and into the institution of the Parliamentary Commissioner or 'Ombudsman'. At the Community level, while the European Court covers some of the functions of the 'Ombudsman', there is a great deal of scope for action by members of the EP in response to constituency correspondence. And it is possible that the right to petition might become a potent instrument for focusing public opinion on issues with which the orthodox party system cannot cope – say, nuclear energy. In this way the EP could open up new channels of communication and representation both for individuals and for pressure groups.[17]

17. See also Sir Derek Walker-Smith's *The Case for a European Ombudsman*, published by the Conservative Group in the European Parliament, Luxembourg, 1978.

The EP should also aim to develop its Committee system to provide an increased number of 'hearings' open to the public and the media – a procedural device which would incidentally help the Parliament to deal with the problem to which we referred above of its relations with the economic and social interest groups. 'Hearings' are essentially meetings of the EP's Committees in which invited 'witnesses' take part: should the EP acquire a right of subpoena or to 'send for persons and papers' it is obvious that they could become a powerful instrument for inquiry and debate. We shall return to this question in our discussion in the next chapter on the Parliament's procedure and practice.

Finally, the nature of the electoral systems for the European elections is likely to be of determinative significance. The closer a member is to a specific territory and the less he owes to a national party machine – as, for example, under the single-member constituency system which has been adopted in Britain – the more open will be the prospect of the development of a new European form of politics. And the more centralized the system and the greater the hold of the national parties – as under the national list systems adopted in most of the continental member states – the more difficult will it be for such a development to take place. No doubt this consideration will be found at the heart of the debate which must take place in the first directly elected Parliament on its proposals for a uniform electoral system for the whole of the Community.

Chapter 4: How the Parliament Works

This chapter is about the EP's procedure and practice. These are dry matters, but they are of fundamental importance – especially for an institution as young and as innovatory as the European Parliament. Indeed it must be the interaction of procedures with formal powers, exploited by strong personalities, which will give the EP the dynamism and colour it will need if it is to win its share of public attention and achieve results. Thus we have already noticed how the control of its own procedures has enabled the Parliament to improve upon the limited range of functions ascribed to it by the Treaties – for example Question Time, which stems from an imaginative application by the Parliament of its Treaty power to ask questions of the Commission and the Council. Similarly the provision for systematic hearings by the Budgets Committee on Commission proposals with financial implications has forced the Commission to improve the quality of its budgetary forecasting and has enabled the Parliament to begin to put its formal budgetary powers to serious use.

It is also particularly important for British readers to grasp the basic features of the EP's procedures because they differ so much on so many essential points from those with which we are familiar at Westminster. Unlike Westminster – or at least the House of Commons – the EP works primarily through specialist Committees meeting in private; the debates on the floor of the House are less important and less lively than at Westminster. The function of Rapporteur is unknown to British parliamentary politics – except perhaps in the case of a member in charge of a private member's bill. And the parliamentary parties ('Groups' in the EP) are given formalized procedural advantages and staff and facilities on a scale unknown at Westminster. These are the main differences which

83

we will find emerging from our discussion in this chapter of how the European Parliament actually works.

Continuity after Direct Elections

Our topic is best approached by considering the procedures and practice of the present indirectly elected EP. Over the quarter-century since it began, the EP has built up its own traditions and a parliamentary style which owes something to each of the member states' traditions but which differs from all of them. The elected Parliament will have to develop from these foundations – for a number of circumstances point towards continuity rather than change its conduct of business. Not least, the elected EP will be under pressure to resume business as usual without delay. Requests for opinions already on the table will have to be processed, and the Community budget for 1980 will have to be adopted according to the timetable. These pressures will give the EP, once elected, little or no time in the short term to reflect on procedural change in the abstract. At the same time, there will be few Members holding a 'dual mandate', and many Members new to parliamentary politics; and although most Members will be different, the EP's officials will be the same.

Perhaps one of the chief influences on the working of the new EP will be the continuation for the indefinite future of its present pattern of migration between three and more centres of operation. For the EP has not yet acquired a fixed site. In 1967 a complicated political package-deal – of the type perhaps too familiar in the Community – confirmed the continuing decentralization of the Community insti-tutions. The Commission has departments both in Brussels and in Luxembourg. The Council meets in both capitals. And the Court of Justice, the European Investment Bank and the new Audit Court are in Luxembourg. The Parliament has three 'working sites' – Luxem-bourg and Strasbourg for plenary sessions, Luxembourg for its Secretariat and Brussels for most Committee meetings.

The legal status of this decision as to the 'provisional' sites of the EP is such as to put it beyond the Parliament's competence to change it: it flows from an agreement among the member states rather than from a Community decision. On the other hand the Parliament's budgetary powers are now such that it could probably decide unilaterally to vote the funds for a new site. Whether or not it would be realistic to make the attempt depends upon a political judgement, which must in the first place depend on the question of the attitude of the prospective host government to such a move. A wider political consideration is whether the Community is yet ready for the degree of centralization that would be implied by the permanent establishment of the Parliament at a single place. Brussels may be destined to become the Community's Washington, but Europe is still a long way from being a United States. Inconvenient and faintly ridiculous as it may be, it is probably still appropriate that the EP should have not one but a number of centres and that its Members should continue to be obliged to maintain their principal residence in their home countries.

Meanwhile it seems probable that at least for its first year the new Parliament will be holding its plenary sessions in Strasbourg, where the existing Council of Europe building can seat 410 members – unlike the Parliament's present chamber in Luxembourg. The government of the Grand Duchy is pressing ahead with a new building, but this is unlikely to be ready before June 1979. Committee meetings will, however, probably continue to be held in Brussels from the beginning of the new Parliament, if a new building being put up by the Belgian government – on a site too constricted to be adapted for the holding of plenary sessions! – is ready by September 1978.

At present the EP meets on average for fifty-eight days each year. Each month, except in August, it generally holds one 'part-Session', or meeting in plenary, over four working days – from Monday afternoon to Friday noon – as well as an occasional 'special Session' to deal with the budget, lasting between one and three days. As we have seen, the dozen or so 'part-Sessions' each year are held in Strasbourg four or five times a year and otherwise in Luxembourg, where the EP's Secretariat is located. Each of the present twelve specialized Committees meet in Brussels on average twice each month. In addition there is, by tradition, one full week of Committee meetings in Rome each year; and an occasional

Committee meeting takes place elsewhere outside Brussels – for example the Political Committee and the Budgets Committee hold periodic meetings in the capital of the country currently holding the Presidency of the Council of Ministers. Delegations of the EP also travel to meet the Greek, Turkish and American and Canadian parliamentarians with whom 'mixed parliamentary committees' have been formed; and (twice a year) there is a meeting of the 'parliamentary consultative assembly' of the Lomé Convention, with the site alternating between Europe – usually Luxembourg – and one of the associated countries.

Direct elections and the doubling of the numbers of European parliamentarians – most of whom will be full-time – will probably not make much difference to this underlying pattern, although the EP's work will inevitably expand and be intensified. Plenary sessions will probably increase to cover seven or eight working days each month in Strasbourg and, eventually, in Luxembourg – there is already quite enough work to justify this. Committees will meet more often, and they will probably tend to meet more frequently at the same time as plenary sessions outside Brussels – although most Committee work will continue to be done in Brussels because of the location there of the main departments of the Commission. Meetings of the political Groups, which will be at least as frequent as they are at present, will also have to be fitted in. It is likely that one week in each month will be left free of official parliamentary business so that Members will be able to attend to their constituencies. The pattern of work is likely to be such as to require Members to spend some four nights a week for three weeks a month away from home – a commitment whose onerousness should be well understood by everyone concerned.

The Parliament's Officers

The EP's internal structure will be similarly unchanged. Its officers are at present the President, twelve Vice-Presidents, and the Chairmen of the political Groups – which are currently six in number. Together these form the 'Enlarged Bureau', along with the EP's Secretary-General, who is appointed by the Bureau. The

President and the Vice-Presidents are elected each March at an annual constitutive meeting – which will probably take place, after the European elections, in July 1979. Normally a President is re-elected unopposed by acclamation for a second term; but in the alternate years when a new President is to be elected the struggle can be intense and the negotiations between the Groups long and difficult. The present President, Signor Emilio Colombo – a former Italian Christian Democrat Prime Minister – was elected in 1977 only after three ballots (his rival was Mr Yeats of the Irish Fianna Fail, the son of the great Irish poet).

The role of the EP's President lies somewhere between that of the Speaker of the House of Commons – non-partisan and almost non-political but procedurally dominant – and the overtly partisan role of the Speakers of the United States' House of Representatives. The President of the EP does not have the Commons' Speaker's virtually absolute and uncontested right to take major procedural decisions – the calling of amendments, the holding of emergency debates, deciding on the admissibility of questions and so on; but neither is he the leader of the majority party as in the United States. However, he is the representative of the EP and an important symbol of his young and developing institution. The President of the EP also has an increasingly important role to play in leading the Parliament's delegations to the Council under the 'conciliation procedure' described in the previous chapter.

The Vice-Presidents are often former Presidents and elder statesmen wise in procedural matters whose functions are to take the chair in place of the President and to offer procedural advice. Together with the President they form the Bureau, which has a number of primarily administrative functions. However in recent years the Bureau has met less and less and its functions have in practice been taken over by the 'Enlarged Bureau' – which includes, in addition to the President and Vice-Presidents, the Chairmen of the Groups. This body is the nerve-centre of the European Parliament. It adjudicates upon procedural issues, it fixes the draft agenda and it deals with administrative problems and with the long-term planning of the EP's work. It will often ask the advice of the Committee on Rules and Petitions, the Political Committee, or the Budgets or Legal Affairs Committees; but its decision is final, subject to the Parliament itself in plenary session. The most difficult negotiations in the Bureau are usually those concerned with fixing the agendas of the plenary sessions – where the interests of Groups, Committees and Rapporteurs as well as those of the Commission and the Council of Ministers have to be taken into account in arranging debates and in determining the timing of the consideration of questions.

The Political Groups

The political Groups are clearly recognized and established in the EP's Rules of Procedure. Rule 36 states that 'representatives may form themselves into groups according to their political affinity', and numerous other rules refer to them, usually to accord them some procedural advantage over Members acting independently.

Fourteen Members are at present required for a Group to be formed, unless they come from at least three member states – in which case ten is enough. The requirements were originally more strict – a minimum of seventeen – but changes were forced by decision of the Gaullists to sit as an independent force leaving the Liberal Group in 1962, and by the arrival of the Communists in the late 1960s. Recently those members who belong to no Group – one SNP member and the representatives of the Italian MSI – have been accorded secretarial facilities, offices and some choice as to Committee posts. Since the establishment of the Rules and Petitions Committee in 1975, under the chairmanship of William Hamilton, MP, procedural rights have been accorded to *ad hoc* groups of at least ten members, thus improving the position of minorities within the established Groups. But in practice these changes have had little effect on the dominance of the Groups in managing the Parliament's business. This is clearly an issue which will have to be taken up immediately by the new Parliament, which will have at least to fix new minimum numbers even if it does not review the functioning of the Group system – with all the pressures it sets up towards the adoption of multinational perspectives.

It is probable that after direct elections the composition of the EP and the number of political Groups and the balance between them will be much the same as in the present nominated Parliament, which is already reasonably representative of the main currents of politics in the member states. Apart from the Belgian *Volksunie* there is no sizable national political party which is currently denied representation. Incidentally, this has not always been so. In the 1950s and 1960s the French and Italian parliaments selected Members of the EP almost entirely from the majority party or allocated only a token representation to some, but not all, of the opposition parties. The French Socialists were for a long time under-represented during the early years of the Fifth Republic; and the large and powerful Italian and French Communist Parties were excluded – until 1969 in the case of the Italians and 1973 in the case of the French.

At present Members from some forty-nine different national parties sit in the EP (see Appendix A). As we shall see in the next chapter, nearly all of them are associated with one of the six political Groups, of which five represent the main 'political families' which are to be found in the Community. Currently the Groups are: the Socialists – twelve parties from nine member states; the Christian Democrats – twelve parties from seven member states; the Liberal and Allies Group – twelve parties from eight member states; the European Conservative Group – three parties from two member states; the Communist and Allies group – five parties from three member states; and the European Progressive Democrats – three parties from three member states. This last Group does not, however, represent any distinctive political tradition, consisting as it does of Members from the French Gaullist RPR, the Irish Fianna Fail and Mr Mogens Glistrup's Danish Progress Party. There are in addition a number of Members from regional parties – including a single Scottish Nationalist Member – and some from the Italian far-right MSI. These Members do not belong to any political Group.

Since the arrival of the British Labour Party Members in July 1975, the Socialists have become the largest Group, with some sixty-six members; but they are very far from having an absolute majority since this Group consists of no more than one third of the total membership of the present EP. Indeed, no Group has come close to obtaining an overall majority in the EP since the high-tide years of Christian Democracy in the 1950s – when it should be remembered that the nomination procedures tended to favour pro-European and moderate parties of the centre-right.

The Groups are organized on broadly similar lines. Each has a Chairman and a small Bureau in which there normally sits at least one Member from each party and member state represented in the Group. The Group Bureau is responsible for the administration of the Group's business, which is conducted in the first instance by its Secretary-General and Secretariat. Policy is decided by meetings of all the Members of the Group, which are held three or four times during each session – usually lasting about an hour – and once in the week before the Session. At Group meetings a common line is reached on issues coming up on the agenda of the plenary session, a spokesman is appointed with a general mandate, amendments to be moved on behalf of a Group are approved, and the way in which the Group will vote is settled. More generally the Group meetings enable it to develop an overall perspective to serve as a basis for the detailed discussions of particular issues. Longer Group meetings and 'study days' are held twice a year, usually devoted to a special theme which the Group wishes to discuss in depth. These meetings also provide an occasion for personalities from member parties who are not MEPs to take part in the work of the Group. Recently, for instance, M. Chirac and Mr Michael O'Kennedy, the Irish Fianna Fail Foreign Minister, participated in an EPD Group meeting to discuss the European election campaign. Christian Democrat politicians regularly take part in the 'study days' of the Conservative Group, although in the EP the Conservative and the Christian Democrats sit in separate Groups.

It is in the nature of a multinational Parliament with a wide variety of ideological backgrounds and parliamentary traditions among the Members – even those in the same Group – that party discipline tends to be weaker and more difficult to enforce than in national parliaments. Group decisions as how to vote at the end of a debate can hardly be obligatory. The right to dissent is therefore respected in each of the Groups, and usually its statutes simply require a Member to inform the Group meetings if he intends to vote differently from his colleagues. In any case the Groups have no powerful sanctions to bring to bear on a dissident Member: at this stage the most effective disciplines would be those applied by a Member's party at home – and it may well be that a dissenting position in the EP which would make a Member unpopular there would only serve to enhance his popularity at home: for instance views expressed by Labour Party Members of the Socialist Group on the Common Agricultural Policy. This is undoubtedly a difficulty which the European party Groups already face; and it is one which will continue to challenge them, perhaps even more strongly, after direct elections.

The structure, organization and functions of the Group Secretariats are broadly similar. Each is headed by a Secretary-General who enjoys considerable freedom in day-to-day decision-making. At present the Secretariat of the larger Groups consists of up to twelve administrative-grade officials, and the smaller Secretariats usually have about six. One of these is normally responsible for relations with the press and other media, and in some Groups a staff member acts as assistant to the Group President; the others follow the work of one of more of the EP's Committees. In this connection their task is to provide position papers and briefing for their Members on issues coming before the Committees and plenary sessions. They have to keep in touch with the Committee Secretariats, with their opposite numbers in the other Group Secretariats, with officials of the Commission and Council of Ministers responsible for particular areas of policy, and with representatives of professional organizations and interest groups who may provide alternative views or additional information which may be of interest to their Members. Maintaining links with national party organizations – especially with party research departments – is one of their most important functions.

The Parliament's Secretariat

The Secretariat-General of the EP employs some 1,600 officials, a large proportion of whom are translators and interpreters – every document and speech has to be translated or interpreted into six languages. The Secretariat is divided into five Directorates-General (DGs). DG I – *Sessional and General Services* – is responsible for preparing the agenda, servicing the Bureau and the Enlarged Bureau, advising the President or Vice-Presidents in the Chair during sittings, for the preparation of the verbatim records of debates and the minutes of sittings, and for the translation of these. DG II – *Committees and Inter-Parliamentary Delegations* – serves the Parliament's Standing Committees, of which there are at present twelve, and its delegations to inter-parliamentary meetings. These Committee secretariats play a very important role in the working of the EP. Each Committee has a Secretary who is assisted by four or five other administrative-grade officials. They are responsible for preparing the agenda of Committees, for ensuring the smooth running of the proceedings, for procedural advice to the Committee and Rapporteurs and for assisting the Rapporteurs in drafting their reports.

DG III – *Information and Public Relations* – is concerned with the EP's public image and with relations with the communications media. It also runs the Parliament's press and information offices in each of the member stage capitals. DG IV – *Personnel and Administration* – runs the EP's administration and recruits and organizes its staff. DG V – *Research and Documentation* – prepares background papers and research material for the various Committees and for the general information of Members: for example, it has recently published a study of the comparative electoral law of the member states which will be very useful when the new EP begins to draw up a common electoral law for the Parliament. It also works with the Directorate-General for Information and Public Relations in preparing material for public information. DG V also has a Legal Affairs unit which is responsible, among other things, for relations with national parliaments.

How the System Works

The best way to understand the working of these various organs of the EP and the precise manner in which they relate to one another is to follow the progress of a particular legislative proposal through the parliamentary maze. Indeed, as we saw in Chapter 3, one of the EP's main activities is the preparation and delivery of opinions on the Commission's proposals for Community legislation.

When the Parliament receives a proposal from the Commission the President must allocate it to one of the twelve Standing Committees, which will then be considered to be 'in charge' of the proposal. Where the matter under consideration requires it, other Committees may also be asked to give an opinion to the main Committee – thus the Budgets Committee and the Legal Affairs Committee are often asked for specialized views on the financial or legal aspects of proposals. In order to speed up the flow of business, a recent rule change has made it possible for Committees to choose between two possible courses when they receive a proposal. For minor, routine or repetitive proposals – most frequent in the fields of trade and agriculture – a 'no-report' procedure may be adopted. The Chairman and the Secretariat sift through proposals to select those suitable for such treatment, and if there is no objection from any member of the Committee the matter goes forward to the plenary session without a report or debate in the Committee. On the first day of the next session, the President of the Parliament reads out the title of the proposal. If no Member objects to the use of this procedure between then and the end of the session – which normally falls on the Friday morning – the President will declare that a favourable opinion has been given. A single objection returns the matter to the Committee for substantive treatment.

On more important issues the Committee appoints a Rapporteur to draft a report and to lead the debate both in Committee and in plenary session. In the European Parliament Rapporteurs are very important figures who are not found at Westminster. A Rapporteur is a Member who is put in charge of drafting a report and steering it through all stages of discussion. Since the Members cannot hope to study every matter in detail they rely on the Rapporteur to do so, and this gives him considerable leverage in the Committee. His position is a subtle one because he serves not in his own personal capacity but rather as a servant of the Committee – which means that his report must reflect not so much his own views as the views of the majority or of a consensus in the Committee. However, by the exercise of political skills the Rapporteur can have considerable room for manoeuvre in forming the Committee's views – and indeed it will be his first draft which sets the frame of the debate. Furthermore, both in Committee and at plenary sessions he has certain procedural advantages. He alone is allowed to speak at any time and as often as he wishes, and he is always the first to express an opinion on amendments after they have been moved. Furthermore there is a tendency for experienced Members to become virtually the standing Rapporteur on certain issues whenever they come up. Important Rapporteurships are of course much coveted, and they can be the subject of difficult negotiations between the political Groups. The number and the level of Rapporteurs has to be strictly proportioned among the Groups, and Rapporteurships in such important recurring matters as the Budget and the annual farm price review rotate among them. Small wonder, therefore, that with almost no exceptions, the Rapporteurs are chosen only from the political Groups and independent Members are never appointed.

The manner in which a Rapporteur approaches the drafting of his report varies both according to his personality and with the importance of the matter in hand and the extent of his knowledge of it. In any event, in preparing his draft he is supported by one of the four or five officials attached to the Committee Secretariat, and some work on the report may be almost entirely delegated to the Secretariat. Committees sometimes have a preliminary discussion without a written draft, especially in important matters, and on such occasions the responsible Commissioner or a senior official from the appropriate Commission Directorate-General may attend to explain the reasoning behind the proposal, its scope and form, and to attempt to disarm objections before they find their way into the report. Such initial discussion tends to give the Rapporteur some idea of the Committee's thinking, but in the EP as it is at present constituted the absenteeism resulting from the dual mandate may well mean that disagreements continue to emerge at later stages in the proceedings as the composition of the Committee shifts.

In preparing his draft a Rapporteur will probably make contact with Commission officials and with a number of the principal European and national professional organizations and pressure groups – such as the European Trade Union Confederation (ETUC) and the European equivalent of the CBI (UNICE) and the NFU (COPA). At each stage of the discussion Commission officials are present and participating fully in the discussions. They cannot of course either propose or negotiate amendments with the Committee – their position has to be reserved for a collegiate decision by the Commission. But in practice they can exert considerable influence on the Committee, not least because some Members are generally prepared to follow the lead of the Commission unless they have strong reasons for thinking differently. The Rapporteur's contacts with pressure groups are also helpful, whether in giving his report as sound a political basis as possible, or in giving him support for a particular viewpoint which he may wish to espouse, or merely in order to ensure that he is fully informed. Although the EP is neither the only nor indeed the most important focus of political activity in the Community – any more than the national parliaments are at the national level – it is certainly useful for these organizations to ensure that their point of view is given prominence in the conclusions of the report and ultimately in the EP's opinion. For the Parliament can influence the Community's decision-making, and it enables the pressure groups and professional organizations to put their views on record. In this connection there is special value in the 'Hearings' procedure which enables the representatives of organizations to be invited to appear either in public or in private before the full Committee. 'Hearings' have now become a tradition – for example in the Agriculture

Committee's examination of the Commission's annual farm price proposals, when meetings are organized both with representatives of consumer organizations and with the European producer organizations.

After one or two discussions in Committee a consensus or a preponderant view normally begins to emerge. By now the Rapporteur will have a fairly clear idea of whether the Committee wishes to approve or disapprove of the Commission's proposals, and he will therefore know whether his report should be couched in generally positive or in negative terms. He may also have obtained a general idea of what amendments the Committee might wish to see put forward. As discussions proceed these will tend to become more and more technical. Until now the Parliament has rarely refused to support a proposal outright as a matter of principle, and it has been equally rare for dissident minorities which have expressed strong opposition to the Commission's basic concept to go as far as to move amendments proposing a totally negative position: normally the Parliament has attacked the Commission rather for the timidity of its proposals than for going too far or too fast. This instinct may however be modified in a directly elected and therefore more representative Parliament.

Normally the main Committee considering a proposal will have a matter on its agenda at three or four meetings and the other Committees at one or two. But in the present Parliament unavoidable absences caused by the effects of the dual mandate can make the final adoption of a report in Committee a long-drawn-out affair causing the matter to be put off from meeting to meeting. It may also happen that a Committee or some of its Members will seek to use procedural delays to hold up the adoption of an opinion. These were, for example, the tactics of the Socialist and Communist Groups in connection with Lord Gladwyn's report on certain aspects of European defence – which was long held up in the Political Affairs Committee.

Another cause of delay may be the difficulties which arise in reconciling the sometimes divergent points of view of the various Committees. Usually – but not always – before it reaches the final stage of its deliberations the main Committee will have a chance to examine the opinions of any other Committees which have been asked to give their views. The opinions of the Legal Affairs Committee, particularly in respect of the legal aspects of a proposal, and of the Budget Committee in respect of its financial aspects, usually carry considerable weight; but the impact of the views of some of the other Committees may not be so great. It is one of the features of the EP – it resembles the United States Congress in this respect – that much of the political conflict is not so much between nationalities or even between party Groups as between the vested interests and fixed standpoints institutionalized and entrenched in particular Committees. Each of them has built up its own tradition and clientele, and much of the debate in the EP on such issues as the operation of the Common Agricultural Policy, the Mediterranean Policy and the association between the Community and the Lomé Convention countries can best be seen in terms of a conflict between different Committee standpoints which frequently blurs the distinct national and ideological loyalties of their Members. Thus, for instance, when it is considering the Commission's annual farm price proposals the Agriculture Committee is usually loath to give any serious consideration to the views of the Committee on the Environment and Consumer Protection. And there are other examples of inter-committee rivalry.

The final stage of proceedings in Committee is the adoption of a draft resolution. Each report consists of a draft resolution together with an explanatory statement, although the resolution alone is voted upon by the Parliament in plenary session. The resolution may be short – 'the European Parliament approves the proposal of the Commission' – or it may be a long one running to thirty or forty paragraphs. And it will often have to be balanced and even contradictory in order to take account of the views of the various Committees, interests, nationalities and political Groups. Since the EP is consensus-minded, it seeks to avoid close votes and sharp resolutions, and its views often represent only the lowest common denominator of the main Committee – although there is now an increasing and highly desirable tendency towards a sharper definition of political standpoints and therefore towards more conflict.

In part this is due to the arrival of the British delegation with its tendency to transfer Westminster debating styles and party conflicts to Strasbourg and Luxembourg. But in part also it results from the recognition that the Parliament can and must become a more effective political forum in the context of direct elections.

In Chapter 5 we will be considering the questions of the identity and ideology of the political Groups. Here it is interesting to note that in debates at the Committee stage Group standpoints are rare, and normally Members speak for themselves only. This is another reflection of the consensus-mindedness of the Parliament and of the importance of the role of the Rapporteur. Even the Communist Members have adapted themselves to the Rapporteur's role (with which they are in any case familiar from their own national parliaments). And, after some early problems of adjustment, the British Members have also adapted themselves extremely well to the political and procedural environment of the EP. We cannot yet know what the effect of direct elections will be on these reflexes, but it is probably the case that a more 'political' Parliament will witness a tightening of Group discipline. Already the Socialist Committee Members caucus with the officers of the Group Secretariat responsible immediately before Committee meetings; and in connection with some recent issues, such as monetary and economic union and Lord Gladwyn's report on European defence, speakers in Committee have taken up positions on behalf of their Group. It is, however, much more usual to find Members expressing a national or an interest-group standpoint, or a mixture of both. On insurance questions, for example, there are Members who take a particular German view in Committee on the draft Directive on the admission of shares for quotation on the Stock Exchange, while the British Members tend to express the City's view that there should be the minimum public interference in its traditional self-policing arrangements. When the draft Directive on doorstep-selling came before the Legal Affairs Committee in 1977 Members from both British parties turned out in force to oppose harmonization proposals which they considered might interfere with the British practice of mail-order selling.

*

After a report has been adopted, translated and circulated – together with opinions received from other Committees – it remains for the enlarged Bureau to put the matter on the agenda of the plenary session. In this matter, although Committee chairmen and Rapporteurs may be consulted, they do not in fact have much influence on when an item comes up for discussion in plenary.

Once it is on the Parliament's agenda the report will be studied both in the Commission, in most cases also in the Council of Ministers, and in the political Groups. On most major items the Groups will already have defined their views, but the finer points of the Rapporteur's final draft have to be carefully examined. In the nature of things any report is a compromise: what has to be decided at this stage is whether the Rapporteur's final compromise is acceptable. Should a Group spokeman be appointed, and if so what line should he be instructed to follow? Should any amendments be tabled? How should the Group vote at the end of the debate? Although, as we have seen, Group discipline is difficult to enforce and Members who wish to dissent from the Group line may normally do so by indicating their intention in advance, Group solidarity nevertheless remains strong and dissent is the exception rather than the rule.

The debate at the plenary session is opened by the Rapporteur with a general statement outlining his report; Rapporteurs from the other Committees which have also been consulted may follow him. Then the Group spokesmen speak, starting with the largest group – currently the Socialists. Each Group spokesman must normally speak within a time-limit of ten to fifteen minutes, depending on the nature of the debate – for very important debates each Group may be given an increased length of speaking time which may cover several hours. In these circumstances several spokesmen from each Group will take the floor, each of them dealing with some specific aspect of the subject in hand and moving amendments when appropriate. This is how, for instance, debates are organized on such subjects as the Community's budget, the annual farm price review and the Commission's annual programme which is presented by its President in February of each year. After the spokesmen have finished, the floor is thrown open to individual Members – that is Members who belong to no Group, or back-bench Members of the Groups – who are usually subject to a time-limit of five minutes. The Commissioner responsible for the subject matter of the report, or a colleague standing in for him, will generally speak twice in the debate, making a general statement immediately after the Rapporteur has finished, and replying at the end to the debate and commenting upon any amendments which may have been moved. He will normally indicate whether the Commission can accept these amendments. When appropriate the Minister representing the Presidency of the Council (the 'President-in-Office') will also take part in the debate.

All that then remains is for a vote to be taken on the report and the amendments: votes take place only on the motion for a resolution and amendments to it, and not on the report or general explanatory statement attached to it. Under present rules, the Parliament usually votes at certain previously fixed times, usually in the mid-afternoon after Question Time. At the time of voting the Rapporteur alone is allowed to speak briefly to indicate the position of his Committee on each amendment. Voting is normally by a show of hands and roll-call votes are extremely rare – which means that, unlike the situation of Westminster, precise voting figures are not usually announced and are often not available when the show of hands has indicated a clear result. Only the result of the vote is then announced. The total rejection of a report by the EP is rare, though in recent years it has tended to happen more often as the Parliament has become more 'political'. Two significant cases in recent years were the votes in 1975 on a report on the Community's competition policy presented by the British Conservative, Mr Tom Normanton, and that on a report on shipping policy presented by the German Socialist, Mr Seefeld, in 1974. As it happened neither of these were draft opinions in the legal sense – that is to say their rejection did not leave open the question what *was* the European Parliament's opinion on the issue, thus creating a legal void on the question of whether the Parliament had or had not formally given its opinion as required under the Treaties. But to avoid such a possibility arising in the future it has now been decided that the rejection of a report causes the subject to return to Committee. Where there have been numerous amendments, or where amendments adopted in plenary have introduced contradictions into the report, or where the debate has shown that the report arouses fairly general opposition, it may be returned to the Committee for further study and improvement.

Once adopted, the EP's resolutions are sent to the Council and to the Commission, and they are published in the Community's *Official Journal*. Since 1973 the Commission has made a practice of systematically informing the Parliament at the beginning of each session about what it has done to give effect to Parliament's votes in previous sessions. And since 1971 the Commission has amended its proposals to the Council in the spirit of any of the Parliament's opinions with which it agreed. This means that the Parliament's amendments may become part of the basic proposal of the Commission on which the Council must deliberate and decide; and, as we saw in the last chapter, one effect of this is that such amendments can then be rejected by the Council only by a unanimous decision (Article 149 of the Treaty). The Parliament's opinions also form part of the dossier of the Council, of its working parties and of the meetings of the Committee of Permanent Representatives (COREPER); and normally Council bodies do not begin serious work on a Commission proposal until they have received the Parliament's opinion. Of course nothing obliges the Council to accept these opinions, and normally they are no more than one element among many in its deliberations; but as we saw in Chapter 3, growing weight must be attached to the Parliament's opinions on matters which would later require it to vote funds – for these are matters which are subject to the 'concertation procedure' under which Parliament meets the Council and the Commission to press its point of view.

Procedure for Scrutiny and Control

This completes our discussion of the way in which the Parliament participates in the Community's legislative process. We turn now to the procedures through which it exercises its powers of scrutiny and control.

One of the most important and exciting developments in this sphere has been the introduction of Question Time in 1973. This was inspired primarily by the example of Westminster – although it was introduced before Britain joined – and it is still the British and Irish members who make the best and most effective use of Question Time. Initially one hour per part-session was allotted but currently there are two sessions of forty-five minutes each on Tuesday and Thursday, devoted to questions to the Commission, and a period of one and a half hours on Wednesday devoted to questions answered by the President-in-Office of the Council. He will also answer questions, in his capacity as President-in-Office of the Conference of Foreign Ministers, in respect of political co-operation or the co-ordination of foreign policy. Each Member is limited to one question per institution and the closing day for questions to both Commission and Council is Wednesday of the previous week. Questions must be short and in interrogative form, and they may not ask for detailed statistics – but the EP's Rules of Procedure relating to questions are by no means as strict as they are at Westminster. After the initial reply from the Commission or the Council the questioner may ask a supplementary question, and at the discretion of the Parliament's President two or three other members may then ask supplementary questions. Some fifty substantive questions are normally answered in this way by the Commission and the Council at each session; those that remain unanswered are either automatically given a written answer or, if the questioner prefers, they may be postponed till the next session.

The Parliament's Rules also provide for two other types of oral question: urgent questions may be raised under an emergency procedure somewhat similar to Standing Order No. 9 debates in the House of Commons; and oral questions may be put down for debate.

Emergency debates may be held at the request of a Group if, during Question Time, a reply is judged unsatisfactory or if issues of importance are raised which cannot be dealt with satisfactorily under the rather summary Question Time procedure. An hour is set aside for the debate, which follows immediately after Question Time. No motion may be presented. Since it was instituted in

1973 this procedure has only been used four times (twice in relation to Spain, once over milk and once on steel); no doubt in the new Parliament, concern for topicality will cause it to be more extensively used.

Meanwhile a more favoured device has been the 'oral question with debate'. These are more elaborate questions than are admissible at Question Time, and they must normally be tabled by a Group with the approval of the Enlarged Bureau. Under the procedure the questioner introduces his question and the Commission or the Council reply. A short debate then takes place; and a resolution may be tabled to conclude the debate. It has become normal for four or five questions in this form to be asked at each part-session.

Another type of parliamentary scrutiny is afforded by the procedure for asking written questions, which now number in the order of 1,500 each year. Written questions may be asked of both the Commission and Council; the Commission having one month to reply and the Council two months. Written questions are a useful source of information to Members and through them to the public, and they make it possible to raise issues which can then be pursued in other ways. Some Members have made a speciality of asking written questions. The Dutch Socialist Henk Vredeling – an MEP from 1958 to 1973 and currently a member of the Commission – sometimes asked as many as 60 per cent of the questions in a year, thus earning for himself the nickname 'Vrageling' (*vragen*=to ask). A British Member, Lord O'Hagan, topped the table in his period: he is even said to have placed an advertisement in the press asking for material for questions.

The Parliament's scrutiny of the work of the Commission and the Council is largely exercised through its procedures for asking questions and arranging debates; its powers of control are embodied in the procedures by which it may vote to dismiss the Commission, and in its budgetary procedure.

As we saw in Chapter 3, the EP's power to dismiss the Commission requires a two-thirds majority of the votes cast, provided that this amounts to a majority of all Members. In addition the Rules of Procedure require that a censure motion may not be debated until at least twenty-four hours have elapsed after its tabling, and a further forty-eight hours must pass before the vote.

Since the EP first sat in the 1950s only four such motions of censure have been tabled – all of them since December 1972. In that month M. Georges Spénale, a French Socialist and later President of the Parliament, tabled a motion in protest against the Commission's failure to honour an undertaking to present new proposals to increase the Parliament's budgetary powers. The Malfatti/Mansholt Commission was to reach the end of its term three weeks later and the political Groups sought to avoid a vote on this motion, which was eventually withdrawn in favour of a resolution condemning the Commission. Although M. Spénale was serving as the Chairman of the Budgets Committee, his motion of censure stood in his own name. This was also the case with a motion put down by Herr Aigner in 1976, again just before the end of the Commission's term of office. As Chairman of the Control Sub-Committee Herr Aigner was seeking – successfully in the event – to bring pressure to bear on the Commission to make certain documents available to this sub-Committee. The fact that these two censure motions were tabled without the support of a political Group has since led to the introduction of a new rule which requires censure motions to be tabled either by a Group or by a number of Members not fewer than a tenth of the Parliament's total membership.

The two other censure motions that have been tabled since 1972 are of this more formal type. One was moved by the Conservative Group and the other by the European Progressive Democrats. Both concerned aspects of the agricultural policy, and in both cases the motions were heavily defeated.

Censure motions are, obviously, exceptional events. By contrast the exercise of its powers of budgetary control dominate the life of the EP every year from September through to December.

Figure C: The Community's annual budgetary cycle and the role of the EP in it

1st stage	Commission	Preparation of preliminary draft (i) Establishment of maximum rate. Informing the institutions of this rate before 1 May. (ii) Compilation of preliminary draft from budgetary estimates made by Institutions; preliminary draft sent to the Council before 15 June.
2nd stage	Council	First reading: establishment of draft by a qualified majority; draft sent to European Parliament before end July.
3rd stage	European Parliament	First reading: proposal of modifications and amendments within forty-five days.

Compulsory expenditure: Modifications proposed by normal majority	*Non-compulsory expenditure:* Amendments by a majority of members.

4th stage	Council	Second reading decision on proposals and modification of amendments within fifteen days.

Compulsory expenditure: Decision by qualified majority: proposals that are not accepted are considered to be rejected.	*Non-compulsory expenditure:* Modification of amendments by a qualified majority.

5th stage	European Parliament	Second reading: decision on the Council's modifications of amendments and formal adoption of the budget within fifteen days.
		Non-compulsory expenditure: Amendment of Council's modifications by a majority of members and three-fifths of votes cast.
		Formal adoption or rejection of the budget.

The Community's annual budgetary cycle and the Parliament's role in it are set out in Figure C. The procedure – on which we touched in Chapter 3 – may be summarized as follows. Each spring the Commission fixes – by means of statistical calculations based on the rate of growth of the European economy – the maximum rate of increase of the budget for the next financial year beginning on 1 January. This will be the 'margin for manoeuvre' both for the Council and for the Parliament in the coming budgetary discussions. At the same time the Commission sends to Council and Parliament general guidelines as to the size and distribution of the budget for the coming year. These will be debated by Council and Parliament, thus setting the broad framework for the ensuing debate.

Before the end of the summer the Commission completes its preliminary draft budget. This is discussed by the Council and sent to Parliament in late August or early September. Parliament then has some forty-five days to subject this draft budget to rigorous examination. This it does by asking each of its Committees supervising the various areas of Commission spending to submit its opinion to the Budgets Committee. The Budgets Committee will hold eight or nine meetings over the two-month period, and it usually has to consider in a very short period of time several hundred extremely technical and complicated amendments. At the same time it has to arbitrate between different potential uses for the limited resources which the Community has at its disposal. There will be arguments between the differing claims of regional policy, nuclear research, aid to non-associated countries in the Third World, structural reform in agriculture and so on. At the end of this process, Parliament will vote upon the budget and amend it at a special budgetary session which normally takes place in Luxembourg over three days in early October.

The budget then returns to the Council for a second reading, which takes account of the Parliament's proposed amendments. The Council must decide whether, in the area of 'obligatory expenditure', it is prepared to accept them. The President-in-Office of the finance ministers of the Council – that is the finance minister of the country exercising the Presidency – will then appear before Parliament to present the Council's reaction to the Parliament's budgetary positions. At its December session the Parliament must make the final decisions. It may simply take note of the Council's decisions on its proposed amendments to 'obligatory expenditure'. It may, on the other hand, decide to stand by its amendments to 'non-obligatory expenditure' over which it has the last word within the 'margin for manoeuvre'. And it must finally make a general political appreciation as to whether it has received sufficient satisfaction in the budgetary procedure. If it has it will vote the budget. If it has not it may decide to use its power to reject the budget as a whole – requiring that the process be recommenced so that the Council and the Parliament would have to agree on a new budget.

Such a decision would, of course, herald a major political crisis in the Community;[1] but the Parliament's influence in the process does not depend upon this threat. Throughout the budgetary process it is in constant contact with the Member of the Commission responsible for budgetary affairs, with Commission officials from the Directorate-General for budgetary matters, and with the Council of Ministers at both official and ministerial level. Here, as in

1. Michael Shaw, MP (Conservative), has published a first-class account of the Parliament's work on the budget as seen from his position as Rapporteur on the budget for 1978 in his *The European Parliament and the Community Budget*, published by the European Conservative Group in Luxembourg.

every other area of the Parliament's activities, it is the opportunity to persuade, to argue and to expose that is essential.[2]

An Assessment of how the Parliament Works

Our discussion in this chapter of the European Parliament's procedures is based on the assumption of continuity after direct elections. The Parliament's procedures have been in constant evolution. At the time of Britain's accession, Peter Kirk, MP, the then leader of the Conservative Group, presented a Memorandum which proposed a wide range of procedural innovations such as urgent debates on the pattern of Standing Order No. 9 debates at Westminster, more Committee 'hearings' and many other similar ideas, some of which have now been adopted. In late 1975 Parliament set up a Rules and Petitions Committee, initially under the chairmanship of William Hamilton, MP, with a mandate to keep the rules under permanent review. There thus exists not only an extensive body of experience on which the new Parliament can build, but also a fund of ideas for procedural development waiting to be drawn upon.

As its procedures evolve, the European Parliament will continue to draw upon the traditions and experience of the national parliaments, and lessons will no doubt go on being learned from practice at Westminster.[3] But the main determinant of the procedure and practice of the EP will always be the specific task it has to perform – which is, in a phase, to maximize its influence in the Community's political process without the support of anything like the

2. The immediate effect of a vote of total rejection would be to freeze expenditure at the level of the previous year, funds being released each month for each activity equivalent to a twelfth of the amount spent on that activity over the previous year. The EP cannot, therefore, totally 'deny supply'.

3. The traffic seems increasingly to be two-way: Westminster has at least as much to learn from Europe as to teach it. Experience of the Committee-centred working methods of the European Parliament – together with the mounting evidence of the failure of the House of Commons to develop an adequate machinery for scrutinizing Community policy – has certainly fed the current movement at Westminster for a radical reform of procedures in ways that will bring the Commons closer to the practice of Strasbourg.

battery of formal constitutional powers possessed by the national parliaments.

It is in this perspective that it becomes easier to understand the differences between the practice of the EP and that of Westminster, and to see the merits of the EP's approach. The Parliament's committee system as it is now and as it might be strengthened and developed in the future, particularly after direct elections, is very well adapted to its purpose. In committee Members can press for, and obtain, a measure of detailed access to policy-making. This enables the EP's Members to be continuously well informed about the issues facing the Community – a feature which, for example, many 'anti-Market' Members of the European Parliament from both Britain and Denmark consider to be one of the most valuable aspects of the Parliament's work. As a consequence debates in the EP can avoid excessive ideological or partisan divisions and be properly informed by an awareness of the best technical information available. For a Parliament whose influence over the 'executive' must depend more upon the ability to win an argument rather than upon 'brute-votes' this is fundamental. Of course in the present nominated European Parliament with the pressures of the dual mandate, Members are not able always to make the best possible use of their opportunities. On the whole, however, the Committee procedure leads to a less confrontational type of debate on issues which are often extremely complicated and technical; and at the same time the existence of the political Groups provides a balancing factor which helps to ensure that divergent political philosophies do play the part they must in the work of a body which is after all an essentially political institution.

For there is of course a danger that procedures such as those upon which the EP is based may give rise to too strong a tendency to seek consensus, sometimes at the cost of incisiveness and clarity and of the Parliament's ability to function as a genuinely informative forum of debate. In the present Parliament sharp political divergences have been avoided and they have been smoothed over as far as possible when they appear. But this can be traced back not so much to the Parliament's procedures as to the character of representation in the present nominated Parliament, whose

Members are often largely self-selected on the basis of their strong European conviction – and to the fact that MEPs do not have a direct and pressing responsibility for their actions in the Parliament either to electorate or to party. Moreover up till now the EP has tended to regard itself not so much as a Parliament in the normal sense with the duty of articulating divergent socio-economic, political and cultural interests, but as a pressure group for further and faster European integration. In this role unity and cohesion has been essential, and it has often been given more importance than clarity and realism in the expression of divergent interests and values.

What impact will the coming of directly-elected Members have on this network of rules and customs by which the EP works? We have already pointed out that sheer force of circumstances will make for considerable continuity in procedure, and that only rather slow and gradual changes are likely. The most obvious and immediate change in the Parliament will be that of size. The directly elected EP will count 410 Members as against the 198 Members of the present nominated Parliament. With the existing twelve thirty-five-Member Committees there would be only 420 Committee seats for the 410 Members – barely one Committee seat per Member. A number of solutions could be adopted: either the Parliament could create more Committees with narrower terms of reference; or Committee membership could be rationed to one Committee per Member, perhaps with some Members – leaders in the political Groups – not sitting on any Committees. Both these solutions have disadvantages. On the one hand, if Members are to be permitted to sit on only one Committee each, the work of the Committees will be greatly intensified. On the other, if more Committees are created better co-ordinating machinery will have to be established to ensure liaison between them.

The second and equally obvious consequence of direct elections will be to make possible a full-time Parliament. Most of the 410 Members will only have a European mandate, and although some of them may for a time also be members of national parliaments, this seems likely to be the exception rather than the rule – and probably after the second direct elections in 1984 such Members will be in a very small minority. It is of course true that MEPs may have a wide range of political obligations at a national and local level in various elected bodies and in their political parties, but their main duty is likely to be to the European Parliament. This will inevitably mean longer plenary sessions and more Committee meetings. Two weeks of plenary session per month are likely as an immediate measure; but it should not be assumed that the directly elected Parliament will in any way want for meaningful and important occupation. Certainly there will not be an immediate growth in the amount of Community legislation – although this has tended to increase rapidly in recent years. But the Parliament will be able to greatly improve and deepen the quality of its work. Parliamentary scrutiny of real quality takes time and effort – and the opportunities for this will be available to the EP for the first time after direct elections. The Parliament will also be able to hold longer debates, particularly on major subjects. The annual debate on the Commission's agricultural price proposals could be expanded to fill a full week; and the debate on the second reading of the Community budget could take up a full two weeks, with particular days being set aside for the consideration of particular estimates such as those for the Social and Regional Funds. Debates could also be more thoroughly prepared – for example by dividing Committee proceedings into two parts: the first devoted to information-gathering by the examination of Commission officials and the holding of public and publicized pre-legislative 'hearings' with representatives of major interest groups as well as experts from Community and other organizations; and the second being the customary discussion of the Rapporteur's draft.

Finally, the Parliament will be able to undertake more background preparation. It could look on its own account at the possible future development of Community policy, and try to help set priorities – a job which badly needs doing in the existing Community system. This would give the political Groups a stronger basis for developing their long-term strategies, and it would also enable the Parliament to develop a sharper cutting edge by which Commission proposals would no longer have to be judged *ad hoc* but could be evaluated against longer-term and more clearly defined political and technical considerations. In this function the Committees would not pre-empt the political Groups in what is their main task – that of determining the political climate in the Parliament – but would assist them in doing this more effectively.

Each new procedure which the Parliament may devise should be developed with these objectives in mind. The EP must above all be cautious in inventing new procedures. Procedural reform should arise out of clearly defined needs and clearly proved inadequacies in existing procedures. The European parliamentary tradition should develop gradually and pragmatically. Above all, in the development of its procedures the Parliament should aim to make possible a thorough-going examination of issues on the basis of the best available expert advice: for this is the necessary basis upon which clear political choices can be made.

Chapter 5: European Party Politics

One of the main themes of this book is that the constitutional role of the European Parliament in the Community's system of government is one thing and that its real political role is another. In defining this role the EP's effects on European party politics will be of fundamental importance.

As we saw in our brief discussion at the end of Chapter 3 of the European Parliament's representative functions, political parties are crucial in the organization of opinion in the nation states of modern Western Europe. They are the vehicles through which electorates are given a coherent political choice between alternative policies, and they are the main instruments through which politicians establish and maintain contact with public opinion. It is probable that, as the Community's political system evolves a life of its own, new forms of political organization may eventually emerge at the European level which are not simply the projection of such established national political forces as the political parties. Nonetheless, for as far as we can now see ahead it seems inevitable that the central role of the parties at the national level will be projected onto the European stage – as it is already in the existing nominated EP, whose smooth functioning, as we saw in Chapter 4, depends so heavily on the work of the party Groups.

This dominance in West European politics of the concept of party as the key link between the electorate and the executive explains why so much effort has been put into the creation of Europe-wide party organizations in the period since December 1974 when the decision was made that the EP should be directly elected.

Although these European party groupings call themselves

different names – they are 'federations', 'confederations' or 'unions' – the basic idea is in each case broadly similar. Their tasks are, on the one hand, to prepare for direct elections – that is to provide at the European level a coherent Socialist, Liberal or Christian Democrat standpoint in the election – and on the other to establish machinery for the control of the parliamentary Group in the EP and for co-ordination between it and the national parties.

There are three European party organizations currently in existence: the Confederation of Socialist Parties of the European Community, the European Peoples' Party, and the Federation of Liberal and Democratic Parties in the European Community. There is also the recently established European Democrat Union, which seeks to serve as a rallying point for the forces of the centre-right in a somewhat looser alliance than has been formed among the Socialists, the Christian Democrats and the Liberals. Each of these organizations has grown up since 1974, although each developed out of earlier efforts at co-operation. The three main European party organizations and to a lesser extent the European Democrat Union have very similar structures, procedures and objectives. Although they each tend to a federalist pattern of organization, in practice none of them has much autonomy from the national parties. Each has drawn up, or is drawing up, a 'platform' for the European elections; and each has encountered broadly similar problems of ideology and identity, although the seriousness of the difficulties has varied.

The Socialists

The Socialist parties of Western Europe have a long history of trans-national co-operation, mostly on a somewhat pragmatic and informal basis. The Socialist International was founded in 1864. It held its first post-war congress in Frankfurt in 1951. Currently it has some thirty-three full member parties, mostly from Western Europe, and a number of observer parties. In recent years meetings of its Bureau have been accompanied by informal summits of Socialist leaders from the Community, and European issues have often dominated these meetings.

There have also been attempts to create left-wing European movements, transcending the national parties. The Movement for the Socialist United States of Europe, which was launched by the British Independent Labour Party in 1947, subsequently changed its name to the Socialist Movement for the United States of Europe and took its place in the much more broadly based European Movement. It gave birth in 1961 to the more structured 'European Left', which now has some ten national sections, holding periodic congresses. Since the early days of the Community, a Conference of the Socialist parties of the European Communities has existed, and in this connection in 1958 a 'Liaison Office' was set up, changing its name in 1971 to the Office of the Social Democratic Parties of the European Community.

In the 1960s a number of leading Socialists such as Messrs Mansholt and Vredeling from the Netherlands and René Montant from France reached the conclusion that precisely because direct elections were not an immediate political possibility – because of the attitude of General de Gaulle – the Socialist parties needed to intensify their co-operation in order to move the Community in a Socialist direction. This required a more radical approach which would take the parties beyond the timid system of inter-party co-operation, which they felt to be unsystematic and lacking in the capacity to take binding decisions. Heer Vredeling argued that the parties were as nationalistic and 'sovereignty-conscious' as the governments, and that they were adapting less rapidly to the new trans-national realities than the business world. There was, he complained, no 'common market of political parties'. In this spirit, he and his associates sought to create a European Progressive Party which would have a shock effect on existing structures. An action committee for a European Socialist Party was formed in 1968. This later became the Committee for the Creation of a Federation of European Socialist Parties – a change of name which showed how the original concept was being watered down.

At the same time, the official inter-party machinery took up the question under the impetus of this debate – which, as we shall see, was also going on at the same time in the Christian Democrat and Liberal camps. The idea of a more integrated European Socialist approach ran into a double opposition: from the existing national parties – and particularly the German SPD – and from those who argued that the proposed action would be meaningless until there existed a sufficiently large quantum of power at the European level to permit a European party to carry out the traditional functions of a political party. In the face of these criticisms the federalist initiatives achieved only a minor success. The 1971 Brussels Conference of the Socialist Parties adopted a very wide-ranging and detailed programmatic declaration; and the Dutch Labour Party congress of the same year called for the holding of a special congress of the national parties leading to the adoption of an emergency programme and the establishment of an eventual 'federative partnership' between the parties. In 1972 the Office of Social Democratic Parties sent out a questionnaire to the member parties on this issue. This led in due course to the formation in 1974 of the 'Confederation of Socialist Parties in the European Community'.

Thus the looser machinery of 'Conferences' and a 'liaison bureau' became a 'Confederation'.[1] Congresses are to be held every two years, but the founding Congress had not been held at the time of writing – although it is planned for January 1979 in Brussels. Three party leaders' meetings have, however, taken place.

Meanwhile the Bureau – two representatives from each member party and from the Socialist Group in the EP – meets at least four times a year and can issue recommendations to the member parties and statements on topical issues. The Congress can make binding decisions by a two-thirds majority on a unanimous recommendation from the Bureau – a provision which thus gives each party an effective veto. The Confederation has a small three-man secretariat in Brussels.

Currently it consists of eleven member parties, drawn from all

1. The eleven member parties are: The Belgian Socialist Party (PSB/BSP), the Danish Social Democrats, SPD (Germany), Parti Socialiste (France), Partito Socialista Italiana and Partito Socialista Democratica Italiana (Italy), Labour (Ireland), Parti Socialiste Ouvrier Luxembourgeois (Luxembourg), Partij van de Arbijd (Netherland), the Labour Party and the Socialist and Democratic Labour Party (UK).

nine member states; parties from Greece, Portugal and Spain may send observers. The British Labour Party boycotted all Community institutions until after the Referendum in June 1975, and so it did not join the Confederation until early 1976. (Until then it had occasionally sent observers.) But even then it did not participate in the drafting of the platform. Both the 1976 and 1977 Labour Party Conferences adopted resolutions opposing direct elections and at the 1977 Conference a motion supporting cooperation on a Socialist European Manifesto was heavily lost. The reasoning was clearly set out in a National Executive Committee (NEC) statement in 1976: the party's position 'stems from an opposition to further integration and possible political union in the EEC'. The statement continued: 'It therefore follows that the British Labour Party should continue the campaign against direct elections as a manifestation and commitment to greater political union.' But by 1977 the Commons had already given the European Assembly Elections Bill an overwhelming second reading. Recalling its earlier opposition, the Conference reluctantly declared that 'we do not want to let the mounting feeling of dissatisfaction with the EEC go unrepresented at Strasbourg'. Only in May 1978, after the bill had become law, did the NEC formally accept the logic of this position and put it on record that the party would participate in the direct elections; and only then were the necessary administrative arrangements set in train.

After the decision at the European Council in Rome in December 1974 to proceed with direct elections it was felt to be necessary for the Socialist Confederation to draw up a platform on which its member parties could stand in the elections. At a summit meeting of the leaders of the Socialist parties in November 1974 the principle of such a programme was accepted, and subsequently a steering group was set up together with four working parties, respectively on economic policy, social policy, institutions and external policy. It was in this work that the British Labour Party refused to join.

These groups began work in the spring of 1976 on the basis of papers which were usually drawn up either by the chairman or by the secretary. Each group held some three meetings, and a consensus about what should be attempted was rapidly arrived at. It was decided that the proposed programme should emphasize a relatively small number of salient points on which the parties could agree. On this basis it was possible to avoid doctrinal divisions and north/south splits and to concentrate less on ideological aspects and more on practical proposals, particularly in the economic field – with the emphasis on such issues as employment policy. The discussion of institutional questions concentrated largely on the EP's powers and its relationship with the Commission and the Council. The working groups continued their work until the end of 1976, and a programme based on the work of all four groups was adopted by the Bureau in June 1977 in Luxembourg.

This draft manifesto consists of an introduction and three sections: on institutions, on economic and social policy and on external policy. The Socialists are pledged to strive for a 'peaceful Europe with higher standards of freedom, justice and solidarity'. The leitmotiv is the need for comprehensive action at both the national and the European level, where this is needed to meet goals which can no longer be achieved purely at the national level. On institutional questions the draft speaks of the 'progressive coalescence of our countries' and accepts the need for the transfer of new areas of responsibility to the Community, provided that the pursuit of Socialist policies is not thereby hindered. It argues that the EP should be given co-legislative powers with the Council, and the right to approve the appointment of the Commission. The draft supports more majority voting in the Council.

The section on economic and social policy is the most complex and it has been the most criticized. It sets out eight goals for economic and social policy, the whole seeming to have a rather *ad hoc* character: full employment, stability, a fairer distribution of wealth and income, an effective and democratic economic structure, economic democracy, improved social security, better working and living conditions, improved educational opportunities. The very different approaches of the parties to these issues prevented very clear policy prescriptions: often the proposals for realizing the objectives are quite minimal and clearly inadequate.

The basic concept in the section on external relations is that a more independent Europe would be able to play a more positive role in the world. Relations with the United States are described as ambivalent, but based on 'co-operation on an equal basis' and not on 'confrontation'. A normalization of relations with the state-trading countries of the East is called for. The European Security Conference is positively supported: a more independent Europe is 'a factor for détente'. Europe should also be a factor for international solidarity. It should promote more equitable and just relations with the developing countries.

In sum the Socialist draft manifesto – like the others which currently exist – does little more than set out a catalogue of broad themes. In spite of this, and in some cases because of it, the draft immediately came under fire from several parties as they examined it. Before long a consensus – for a time strenuously resisted by the Dutch – developed that a shorter and more incisive statement was needed, which might serve as a guideline for the drafting of complementary national manifestos. The French party took no clear position, because of their national elections in March 1978, but there was strong criticism of the draft in the PS as 'social democratic' and in contradiction with the party's policy on Europe as defined at its Special Congress on Europe at Bagnolet in December 1973. The Dutch PvdA Congress proposed some thirty amendments, on issues such as quality of life and energy policy. The Irish and Danish parties each tabled their own proposals for a shorter statement. The British Labour Party took no official position, but it appeared to regard the draft as too federalist and lacking in concrete Socialist policies. Only the SPD and the Luxembourg PSOL and, with some nuances, the Italian parties gave their approval.

So it was that the party leaders' meeting held in Brussels in June 1978 approved a short thirty-one-point 'Political Declaration'. The draft manifesto is to be reworked in the light of this text and of the other amendments, and presented to the Confederation's first Congress in January 1979. All parties have agreed that these two texts will be regarded as guidelines to be used by the member parties in drafting their own national manifestos, which must not be in contradiction to the 'European texts'. The Political Declaration is a balanced document: it refers to the need to promote Socialism both on the national and European levels, it sets out a Socialist critique of the development of the Community to date, noting with concern for example 'the inability of the present social structure to solve the grave problem of unemployment' and condemning 'uncontrolled economic growth'. It fixes the goals of the Socialist parties: 'the pursuit of the common goals of freedom, social justice, equality and harmonious economic development'. New policies are proposed to give priority to the fight against unemployment and to democratize economic power structures. The individuality of each party is explicitly recognized. And these institutional proposals are very prudent: 'the directly elected Parliament must initially develop within the framework of the existing Treaties'.

The Christian Democrats

An early attempt at trans-national co-operation among Christian Democrats was the foundation of the Nouvelles Équipes Internationales (NEI) in 1947. The Christian Democrat parties as such were not directly represented in this organization; rather it was made up of national 'teams' in which a number of parties could participate along with representatives of other groups, including trade unionists. This movement led in 1961 to the formation of the World Union of Christian Democrats (UMDC) and of the European Union of Christian Democrats (UEDC) in 1964; the regional centres of UMDC are formed by this body, together with the South American Christian Democrat Organization (OCDA). A series of *ad hoc* conferences of presidents and secretaries-general of Christian Democrat parties in the EEC has been held since 1958, and these were brought under the UEDC umbrella in 1970. In April 1972, this arrangement was transformed into the Political Committee of the Christian Democrat Parties of the European Community, and it was given a formal status as part of the UEDC structure.

The Christian Democrats have felt the impact of the same type of reform movement as we have described in the Socialist camp; and here also it was led by a Dutchman, Heer Theodorus Westerterp. He launched the idea of a 'European Peoples' Party' at a meeting of the Dutch branch of UEDC in June 1970, and argued that the existing 'co-operative' rather than 'integrated' structure of the UEDC was inadequate because it could not take decisions binding upon its member parties. Under his proposal the existing national parties would be able to affiliate to the proposed European Christian Peoples' Party only if they were willing to accept a common programme and collective discipline. Eventually in 1972, the parties established a joint UEDC–EP Christian Democrat Group working party to examine a common programme.

The November 1973 UEDC congress in Bonn led to an intensification of this drive towards a European party; a new chairman, Herr Kai-Uwe von Hassel of the German CDU, was elected, and seven working groups were set up, including one to draw up the elements of a common programme and another on European Union. Further discussion, and the prospect of direct elections, led to enough progress both on the question of inter-party relations and on a draft manifesto – preparation of which had been in train for some years – to permit the Political Committee in September 1975 to charge a group to draft a statute for a European Christian Democratic party. These statutes and the manifesto were adopted at a meeting of the Political Committee of the UEDC in Paris in February 1976.

The formal establishment of the party was delayed, however, until a meeting in Brussels in April 1976, mainly because of differences over its name – which were in turn symbolic of a deeper divergence over its scope. Some of the national Christian Democrat parties – such as the Italian DC and the Belgian PSC/CVP – were unwilling to include Conservatives and other 'moderates' in the new European party because it might then appear too right-wing. The concept of the new party as an anti-Socialist bloc was plainly unacceptable to national parties which habitually seek support at the national level across the centre and towards the left. For its part, the Dutch Christian Historical Union was unready to dilute the party's Christian commitment with non-confessional Conservatism; while, on the other hand, the German CDU – and in particular its then Secretary-General, Dr Kurt Biedenkopf – sought a broad non-confessional, anti-Socialist alliance, including the Conservatives in Britain and Denmark, which could confront the Socialists on a European scale in direct elections.

A compromise prevailed as to the name: the 'European Peoples' Party – the Federation of Christian Democratic Parties of the European Community'. Different views about the nature of the party were, however, still evident in the speeches made at its foundation meeting in Luxembourg in July 1976. For example M. Charles Fernand Nothomb of the Belgian PSC observed that 'to create a Peoples' Party is to create a political force which seeks to regroup people from all social classes, not merely to bring them in, but to do so to work for a common ideal based on solidarity'; while on the other hand Dr Biedenkopf placed less emphasis on the 'social' vocation of the EPP and more on its openness to the centre-right. 'The EPP,' he said, 'is the basis of a free Europe, but it is not a closed shop . . .' But in spite of these philosophical divergences one firm choice has clearly been made. The statute of the EPP is strongly federal. There is even provision for individual membership. The representation of the constituent parties is weighted according to their strength in the European Parliament, and its organs can adopt binding decisions by majority vote. The party's President and its political bureau have a very wide scope. M. Leo Tindemans, the former Belgian Prime Minister, is the first president of the EPP, and its present vice-presidents are M. André Colin (France), Signor Dario Antoniozzi (Italy) and Heer Schmelzer (Netherlands). Its political basis is the European Christian Democratic Manifesto which was adopted in Paris in February 1976.

A Programme Committee with seven specialized working groups was subsequently established under the chairmanship of M. Wilfred Martens (CVP/Belgium) to draw up an EPP Programme for direct elections, and this draft Political Programme was approved almost unanimously by the first EPP Congress held in Brussels in March 1978. The basis of this Programme is the 'personalist' Christian social tradition, based on the concept of the individual as essentially a social being situated not only within his national society, but also within the European Community and in the community of the whole world. Europe is seen as an essential frame of reference. But it must assert itself – 'Europe can only maintain its personality, its independence and therefore its ideals of freedom, justice, solidarity, peace and democracy, together.' This theme runs through the three main policy sections: solidarity, justice and 'personality' all in balance. There is a section on Europe's place in the world. There follows a section on the policies of the Community (economic life, agriculture, small business, energy, etc.). The EPP seeks 'libertarian and socially just policies based on the effectiveness of the social market economy'. In economic and social life it proposes 'partnership and solidarity'. It approves the Tindemans Report's approach to economic and monetary union. The Programme declares itself for a federal Europe, but, as with the Tindemans Report, its concrete institutional proposals are rather modest: no significant immediate increase in the EP's powers is proposed, and the basic structure of the decision-making process of the Community is accepted as it now is. The Parliament is simply 'expected to bring new constitutional and institutional impulses towards European Union'. The only really new proposal is to associate the regions of the Community with decisions which concern them.

The main problem for the twelve Christian Democrat parties in the EPP is not, however, that of drawing up a programme – which did not in the event present many difficulties, since it was conceived more as a general statement of principles than as an election manifesto. The real issue for the parties in the EPP are those of identity and strategy. They must eventually make a difficult choice between a centre-right alliance and a position of Christian Democrat independence. Different nuances on this issue were evident even in the apparent unanimity of the March 1978 Congress. M. Nothomb (PSC/Belgium) spoke of 'affirming the most important characteristic of our Party: its vocation as an authentic people's party'. He rejected 'splitting our societies into antagonistic blocs which might become irreconcilable in time'. For the Italian Party, Signor Luigi Granelli argued that 'we could never become a party living from day to day in pure pragmatism'. The Dutch CDA representative, Heer Hans de Boer, spoke of 'avoiding fronts of the left or of the right'. In contrast, Herr Frans Heubl of the

German CSU said: 'let us avoid falling into stultifying ideology; the EPP must remain open to all who want to defend freedom in Europe.' And the Chairman of the Programme Committee argued that 'this combination of solidarity and justice with personal freedom is the expression of the originality of the Christian Democrats for whom pluralism and decentralization are not mere words . . . Federalism is an expression of our 'personalist' philosophy. We Christian Democrats stand between right and left. We face them both.'

The Liberals

The Liberal International was founded in 1947 at Oxford. Its membership of about twenty-five parties is largely concentrated in the white Commonwealth and in Western Europe. Liberal parties from the Council of Europe also belong to the 'Liberal Movement for a United Europe'. The basic statements of Liberal principles are the two Oxford declarations of 1947 and 1967. These are both, of course, very general. They centre on the Liberal concern with political and economic freedom adapted to modern conditions; and although by 1967 there was a greater recognition of the need for some state intervention in economic and social life it was envisaged that it would be limited to the strictly necessary minimum.

The 1972 congress of the Liberal International adopted a resolution asking the party leaders to examine the practicality of setting up a Federation of Liberal Parties in the European Community. The reaction was positive and a working party, chaired by Heer Henk Talsma from the Netherlands, was set up and reported to the 1974 Congress at Florence. At this Congress a draft statute was adopted which it was then left to the individual parties to ratify.

The founding Congress of the new Federation of European Liberals and Democrats (ELD) was held in Stuttgart in March 1976. It elected Gaston Thorn, the Prime Minister of Luxembourg, as President of the Federation, and it adopted a 'Stuttgart Declaration'. The German Free Democrats (FDP), Dutch PVV, Belgian PLP/PVV/PL, Luxembourg PED, Danish Venstre and the French Parti Radical and Radical Socialiste Républicain joined from the start. Subsequently, the Italian Liberal Party (PLI) and the Italian Republican Party (PRI) joined, as did the French Radicaux de Gauche. The British Liberal Party Assembly at Llandudno in September 1976 finally ratified British membership; and the French Républicains Indépendants (Giscardians: now the Parti Républicain) joined at the November 1976 Congress. The arrival of the Giscardians caused the British delegation to table a critical motion in the Congress – which was, however, not voted upon. Few imagine that the British Liberal Party will ever reconsider its membership.

The same cannot be said of the French Radicaux de Gauche who responded by 'suspending' their participation and declaring that they would reconsider their position. From the Liberal point of view the whole French scene is in an interesting state of flux; and the National Assembly elections of March 1978 and their aftermath will have important repercussions for the Liberal camp in the long run, although at the time of writing it is too early to say what they might be. The Radicaux de Gauche (MRG) had a poor election, losing two National Assembly seats. This led to a change of leadership. The new President of the MRG, M. Michel Crépeau, is a stronger proponent of an alliance with the Socialists than was M. Fabre, so an immediate return to ELD is unlikely; but he will have to give some thought to asserting the independence and individuality of his Movement. Of much greater potential significance for the reshuffling of the French party pack was the formation, just before the elections, of the Union pour la Démocratie Française (UDF) from three Liberal and centrist formations: the Giscardian Parti Républicain (in ELD), the Radicals (in ELD) and the Centre des Démocrats Sociaux (in EPP). This league was electorally most successful, and it now rivals the Gaullists in terms of both votes and seats. It is becoming more structured and it may well decide to fight direct elections as a unit. One very recent straw in the wind was the tabling of a bill in the National Assembly raising to 10 per cent – from 5 per cent – the electoral threshold for direct elections, which would stop most small parties fighting alone from winning any seats. These moves could have important effects for both the ELD and the EPP.

The ELD held its first Congress at the Hague in November 1976, where the debates centred on papers from working parties on human rights, European institutions, agriculture, economics and finance, regional policy, foreign policy, defence, investment, the standard of living, the role of the self-employed and small and medium-sized businesses, social policy, and energy. At the Hague there was wide agreement on the main outlines of a common programme, but some issues, such as the powers of the elected European Parliament, regional policy, and defence and foreign policy – in particular relations with the United States – required further study. The reports of the working groups were consolidated into a Programme by May 1977 in time for adoption later that year at the ELD's second Congress. M. Thorn was confirmed as president and Herr Hans-Dietrich Genscher of the German FDP – the German Foreign Minister – and Heer Hans De Koster of the Dutch Liberal Party were elected vice-presidents. Among the British Bureau members are David Steel, MP, and Russell Johnston, MP.

The Liberal Programme is more than twice the length of the Socialist manifesto, and it will no doubt be supplemented by a shorter document at the time of the election. It is a mixture of philosophical principles and concrete commitments. Central to the document is the Liberal philosophy of the individual. This idea permeates and binds together the specific chapters, especially those on human rights, institutions and economic policy. Provided that this basic concept is adhered to, a pragmatic and flexible approach to problems is advocated. In institutional matters the Programme unequivocally accepts the concept of European Union. It proposes strengthening and then replacing the existing Community institutions in that perspective. Initially, the EP would be given co-legislative powers and the present 'imbalance between the institutions' would be righted. The Union would eventually be endowed with new institutions: a European government, a Council of States and a Parliament with full powers.

In the economic field, the Liberal Programme places its main emphasis on the urgency of European economic and monetary union, on regional policy – which must take account of cultural diversity and the need for decentralization – and on support for small business, which deserves support as much for social as for economic reasons. In respect of external policy the Programme argues that the European Union should have a common foreign policy which would operate within the framework of the Atlantic alliance and which would also embrace security considerations.

The Liberal Federation faced not inconsiderable problems in drafting its Programme, especially on questions of security, the Atlantic alliance and regional policy. However, as with the Christian Democrats, there are more fundamental problems about the range of views which should be permitted in the Federation. What kind of liberalism does it espouse? – for there are in the Community at least two types: classic liberalism, and 'social' liberalism; and while some Liberals emphasize their lay origin, others do not. Some have traditionally taken part in centre-left coalitions or alliances (the Danish Radikale Venstre, the German FDP since 1969 and the British Liberal Party since 1977), while others have participated in centre-right coalitions (the Belgian, Dutch and Italian parties). One of the key issues, as has been seen, was the admission of the Giscardians — although their members sit in the Liberal Group in the European Parliament. In the result the parties of the Federation now cover a very wide range of views, from the French Radicaux de Gauche on the left – they were co-signatories of the Programme Commun with the Socialists and Communists – to the Benelux and Italian Liberals, passing through the Danish Social Liberals and the British Liberal Party. The Danish Radikale Venstre were, however, unable to accept the Programme and they resigned in 1978.

The most striking feature of the Federation's statute is its extremely federalist character. Binding decisions can be made by a two-thirds majority in the Congress in relation to matters relating to the European Community as such in respect of European Union. Of all the party groupings the Liberals have perhaps the least hesitations about supra-nationality, both in the Community institutions and in their inter-party arrangements. Article 10 makes it clear that the Liberal Group in the EP has an organic link with the Federation, as 'its' political expression in the Parliament. Membership of the Congress is based on the mixed formula of a basic representation of six members per country – shared between parties if necessary – and additional members in proportion to the number of votes obtained in national elections. At the time of writing this last provision ensures that the British Liberal Party has the largest delegation.

The Conservatives and Their Allies

In 1975 the British Conservative Party Conference voted in favour of a 'moderate centre-right alliance' or a 'European Democrat Party'. It is clear that this was a recognition of the danger of entering direct elections without continental allies. Since the 1960s the party has participated in a loose grouping – the European Union of Conservatives – which goes beyond the Community and covers the German CDU and the old French UDR (the Gaullists) as well as the Scandinavian Conservative parties. However, it does not include all Christian Democrat parties, or indeed any Liberal parties. For this reason the former German CDU Secretary-General, Dr Kurt Biedenkopf, pressed for the creation of an 'outer circle' of like-minded parties outside the Christian Democrat EPP.

This would unite in a loose grouping all the various elements of the centre-right: Christian Democrats, Conservatives, Liberals, Gaullists and other 'Peoples' Parties'. From the start the idea was that this alliance would have very little formal machinery, but that it would act in parallel with growing co-operation between the centre-right groups in the European Parliament – especially the Christian Democrat and Conservative Groups.

A meeting attended by Mr William Whitelaw was held in Salzburg in September 1975 to discuss the formation of the European Democrat Union (EDU).

Draft statutes were drawn up for a grouping organized around an initial nucleus of the German CDU, the British Conservatives and a number of other Conservative parties, including some from the smaller European democracies outside the Community. However, to get the arrangement off the ground took almost another three years and considerable pressure both from the CDU's

Bavarian partner – the Christian Social Union (CSU), led by Herr Franz-Joseph Strauss – and from the British Conservatives, who had in the meantime overcome their initial reservations about the scheme. Two more major meetings were held: at Munich in March 1977 and in Salzburg in April 1978. This meeting at last saw the formal foundation of EDU.

The EDU is and will no doubt remain a loose 'working alliance of European centre-right parties' as its founders called it. The Salzburg meeting was attended by a strong Conservative delegation led by Mrs Margaret Thatcher. She reiterated her belief that the creation of an effective working alliance of the centre parties and the Christian Democrats was 'a task of historic importance and one in which we should invest all our energies'. And she went on to insist that '. . . democracy can only be preserved through a commitment to moral values which recognize the unique significance of the individual. In our declaration today we stress the positive beliefs that we share.'

The founder members of the EDU are the German CDU/CSU, the British Conservatives, the Danish Conservatives, the French Rassemblement pour la République (RPR) – the successors to the Gaullists, led by Mr Jacques Chirac – together with a number of Scandinavian parties, the Austrian Peoples' Party and some parties from the 'candidate' countries, Greece, Portugal and Spain. The Italian and Benelux Christian Democrats, however, declined to attend. President Giscard's Parti Républicain – which is a member of the Liberal Federation – also attended as an observer.

These teething troubles illustrate the complexities inherent in bringing together parties and movements with such varied traditions. The absence from the EDU of the larger part of the Christian Democrat movement points to one weakness; the presence of the French RPR points to another – for the RPR is itself the focus of another centre-right grouping. This is the 'European Progressive Democrat' Group in the European Parliament, in which M. Chirac's Gaullists are allied with the Irish Fianna Fail and the Danish Progress Party. In many ways this alliance is no more than a marriage of convenience. But there is a common basis in support for the Common Agricultural Policy, in a pragmatic approach to institutional questions, and in fact that Fianna Fail and the RPR are parties which originated as national movements based on an historic figure who became synonymous with their nation – de Gaulle and de Valera. Such considerations may suffice to keep the EPD Group together; but it does not intend to organize a European party for the elections. However, if the RPR fails to retain the necessary level of support, both in France and at the European level, these three parties should be available to join a Conservative alliance or the wider centre-right grouping of the EDU.

Meanwhile the EDU must overcome the obstacles which arise from the weight of political history and from the hesitations of both its members and its prospective associates. The EPP and the Federation of Liberal and Democratic Parties regard the EDU with some reticence; and what is sometimes regarded in Christian Democrat circles as the brashness of the German CDU/CSU (with their slogan *Freiheit statt Sozialismus* – 'Freedom not Socialism' – which they are seeking to transplant onto the European level) worries parties who naturally gravitate at the national level towards alliances with Socialist parties which are considerably more radical than the German SPD. Moreover, the EDU has the defect of being an essentially Northern European inspiration. Unlike the EPP it follows north–south cleavages in the Community, rather than bridging them. Were it not for recent – and not so recent – political history we could expect a cohesive centre-right group to emerge around the Christian Democrats capable of winning a dominating 120 seats in the European Parliament.

The Communists

The international relations of Communist parties have been strong ever since their emergence under Leninist inspiration in the 1920s; but until 1959 there were no West European regional organizations nor any regional conferences. Even now, the European Communist parties have not established co-operation machinery covering the European Community as such, although bilateral Italian–French (PCI–PCF) relations, as well as the newly established European regional conferences, have been to a large extent dominated by EEC and related issues. No European Communist organization is envisaged for fighting the EP elections.

This is not the place to relate in any detail the development of Communist positions on the Community. The 1962 World Communist Conference in Moscow was important in the EEC context in that it adopted thirty-two 'theses against capitalist integration in Western Europe' which codified the position which the West European Communists had already taken up in national debates on the Coal and Steel Community, the European Defence Community and the Common Market. These consecrated the view that the EEC was an economic arm of NATO and hence an instrument of American hegemony, that the EEC could not increase prosperity, and that it hindered the achievement of socialism in its member states.

However, already at the 1959 Regional Conference, the Italian PCI had tentatively begun a theoretical re-evaluation of the Community; and the 1962 Moscow Conference saw the first signs of open Italian dissent. The party chairman, Signor Luigi Longo, told the PCI Central Committee that 'the EEC has become a determinant element in the Italian recovery'; and in the period 1966–9 the Communist trade-union confederation (CGIL) and the PCI sought and obtained representation in Community institutions. In November 1971 Signor Giorgio Amendola, the party's International Secretary, informed the Central Committee that 'a whole new field of initiative and activity for Communists has opened up'. The PCI's goal, he said, was 'the democratic transformation of the Community from the inside'. In this spirit the PCI has played a constructive role in the European Parliament, and it has made serious attempts to define a wide-ranging European policy.

The main axis of the Communist movement in Europe is the PCI–PCF, who are the only parties enjoying a significant national position. Their co-operation is all the more important in the absence of any formal organization at the European level. There are, however, serious differences on European questions between the two parties – with the PCF opposed to supranational institutions and indeed to direct elections. On economic matters, there is a convergence of analysis but not of policy conclusions: the PCF favours a return to national 'economic sovereignty' and nationalization as a counter to the 'monopolies', whereas the PCI favours countervailing Community-level control. At a recent conference in Brussels M. Marchais told the press that 'we exclude the idea of a single decision centre for the European or world Communist movement; the conference has created no secretariat nor any other common organization at European level'. This remains the firm position of the Communist parties.

The Problem of Accountability

There is no doubt that the emergence of the European political groupings which is described in this chapter is impressive and pregnant with significance for the future. But these tendencies are still very recent – and the newly-founded European political groupings consequently lack the depth and density of identity which marks their constituent parties at the national level.

This lack lies at the basis of one of the most frequently heard objections to direct elections – that it is a sham exercise in democracy because the elected members will not be accountable to their electors. The electors, so the argument runs, will not really know what they are voting for or about and the European MPs will not be subject to the kind of control and discipline that a properly developed party system affords.

The accountability of elected representatives to their electors is of course one of the cornerstones of our democratic system – although it must be admitted that it does not always work as well as it should in national politics. At the national level there is long-standing constitutional and party machinery to ensure such accountability. At the European level, on the other hand, in spite of the European party organizations whose development we have just described, no such machinery yet exists. It will therefore have to be invented in a situation which is much more complex than that which exists in national politics.

Until now the problem has not been pressing because the Members of the European Parliament have been members at the same time of their national parliaments. They have therefore been accountable to their parties and electorates at the national level in the normal way; but from this point of view their membership of the EP has been something of a side-show. The Members have of course depended on their parliamentary parties for nomination to the European Parliament, but otherwise there has tended to be a vacuum in respect of accountability for their European activities. Indeed Heer Henk Vredeling, the long-serving Dutch Socialist MEP, now a Commissioner, has remarked that in fifteen years in the European Parliament he was never held to account for his actions there by his party at home.

With direct elections this will change – if only because of the fact of election itself. The MEPs will need to feel firm political ground beneath their feet – and this, after all, is one aspect of accountability. Although in Britain we are used to the concept that a Member of Parliament owes his electors his judgement rather than his living, all the same it will be particularly difficult to ensure adequate accountability unless imaginative solutions are discovered by the national parliaments, by the parties and by the Members of the EP themselves. Not least among the difficulties will be the large size of the constituencies, whether British-style or regional or, indeed, national; further problems arise from the fact that the European Parliament has only limited powers and can deal with only a limited range of matters. But these features will not make it impossible for the appropriate links – and bonds – to be developed; they will only make it difficult.

Accountability may mean an obligation to take into account the opinions of others, or it may simply refer to the existence of processes of mutual information. Both types of accountability will no doubt be required of the MEPs. Essentially, they will be accountable to their constituency, to their party locally and nationally, and perhaps in some measure to their national parliament. In some member states accountability to a constituency may not be important, but in those countries such as Britain, France and Ireland where there has traditionally been a close local identification between voters and Members of Parliament this kind of accountability will no doubt continue to play a significant part.

On this point it has been argued in Britain that the large amorphous 'Euro-constituencies' will have no clear identity of interests. But in fact the seats which have been proposed correspond to a surprising extent with recognizable existing entities. Bristol, Leeds, Leicester are all single seats. This means that there will often be feelings of local interest and concern which the MEP will need to understand and articulate. Of course the traditional approach to nursing a constituency will not be possible. But as we saw in Chapter 1, the size of European constituencies in Britain will not be much larger than that of congressional districts in the United States. Those who argue that MEPs with such large constituencies are bound to be lost to sight have overlooked the extent to which the American legislator is in practice in many ways more directly held to account by his district than are British members at Westminster. Public opinion can and does work its way through, forcing congressmen to take account of it.

Indeed American methods will be needed. MEPs will need adequate back-up resources. They will need the support of personal staffs, in addition to the existing EP Group Secretariats. The Member will have to spend much of his time out of his constituency – and indeed out of the country – in Brussels, Luxembourg and Strasbourg. He will have to have 'staffers' at the seat of the Parliament to monitor developments there and to undertake research on matters of interest to him, and – perhaps even more important – he will also need them to work in his constituency, to be the first line of communication with individuals and organizations. He will also have to foster links with the local and regional news media: local press, regional and local radio programmes, and television stations.

Much will depend on the way the European Parliament develops. The MEPs will perhaps in the first instance need to create their own 'issues', positively seeking out contacts and publicity. No one knows how much 'case-work' or local representation will fall to them. They will not, of course, have the numerous individual problems which haunt a Westminster member's surgery, and their main contacts will tend to be with well-established local, national and European interest groups. At the same time, however, it should not be forgotten that in many areas with declining industries, such as steel, coalmining, textiles and shipbuilding, or in areas with marginal agriculture or with problems of poor transport infrastructure, the policies of the Community already have a very direct impact on the basic bread-and-butter issues which concern people most directly. They have therefore a direct interest in influencing the various Community policies – the Common Agricultural Policy, the Regional and Social Funds, policies on competition and state aids, the external trade policy. These Community responsibilities have a major impact on jobs and on the standard of living of many areas, and a number of constituencies will have a close identification with certain Community policies – Liège and Charleroi in Belgium and South East Wales with coal and steel, Humberside and Brittany with fishing, Lancashire East with textile imports. These examples could be multiplied: in such areas MEPs will have almost the same localized representational functions as members of the national parliaments.

MEPs will also be accountable to their parties, both locally and nationally. We saw in Chapter 1 how the arrangements for the selection and promotion of candidates are likely to work. The local institutions set up to perform these tasks could supply the basis for a variety of bodies to which MEPs would be expected to report back and which could monitor their performance. In the British Labour Party such arrangements would presumably be based on the decision of the 1977 Party Conference to the effect that 'candidates must be selected before *each* election, using normal constituency machinery, and must be *bound by party policy* and *accountable to the party*' (the authors' italics).

Accountability to the party may exist at the national level too. Indeed, in those countries using the national list system it will exist only at this level. This cuts both ways: MEPs will – as the Labour Party puts it – 'be bound by party policy', but they will no doubt also expect to play a significant part in the determination of that policy. This will mean active involvement and interaction in central policy-making, organized both through party machinery and perhaps through parliamentary procedures. There are many means by which that can be ensured. In Britain MEPs could be admitted to meetings of the Parliamentary Labour Party and the Conservative 1922 Committee: representatives of party delegations could sit in the Shadow Cabinet when their parties are in opposition, or in the Conservative 1922 Executive or the PLP's Liaison Committee when in government. MEPs could attend the specialized back-bench committees which both major parties have set up at Westminster – although perhaps MEPs could only be given non-voting status in these bodies. The parties might also accord MEPs the same rights as national members and candidates in the organs of the party outside Parliament, and especially in the party conferences.

Some parties might seek to go further and impose some obligations to the national party on MEPs – as the Labour Party's policy already implies. At their 1977 Congress the Danish Social Democrats have already approved amendments to party rules dealing with this situation. MEPs are to be subject to general party discipline, they may sit in the party's executive without voting rights, and they may attend meetings of the national parliamentary group. They are required to consult the party executive before all major votes in the EP. It could be argued that such procedures will conflict with European party and Group discipline. But on the other hand to rely on accountability at the European level only at this stage could make accountability wholly illusory. As we have seen, the European Party Organizations are not yet sufficiently developed, and they are in any case still very dependent on the national parties which belong to them.

Nevertheless, difficulties will undoubtedly arise from the fact that MEPs will have to reconcile currents of policy and decisions coming on the one hand from the national level and on the other from the European level represented by the European Party Organizations and the EP Groups. The statutes of the Party Organizations mostly refer to the Groups and accord them some representation in their governing bodies; but they usually do not spell out the relationship between the Groups and the parties – although the Liberal statute refers to Congress 'recommendations to the Group'. No doubt some clarification will be required. In all events, neither the Party Organization nor the Groups can impose significant sanctions on MEPs who do not follow their decisions; and neither are they in any sense vehicles of pressure from below. MEPs will no doubt have to take very seriously policy orientations from all these sources; but when it comes to a decision national party and constituency views will surely tend to prevail.

The relationship between MEPs and their national parliament will also raise problems, as well as opening up avenues for accountability. Some would no doubt like to see Westminster control the MEPs. But such a concept is hardly practical since MEPs will be elected representatives, not representatives of the Westminster parliament.

However, there will be a great deal of scope for procedures allowing for the exchange of information and the avoidance of conflict and misunderstanding, and going beyond the intra-party arrangements we have just discussed. There are various suggestions on the table. In Holland it has been proposed that MEPs should be 'special' members of the Dutch parliament. In Germany the 'Berlin status' arrangements – that is, non-voting status – offer a precedent. Neither of these formulae would probably be acceptable in Britain, even though such eminent parliamentarians as Mr Edward Heath have been prepared to consider them. Other solutions would admit MEPs to use the 'facilities' of the national parliament; and at Westminster the main recommendation of an excellent House of Lords European Select Committee report published in August 1978 was that a Grand Committee of MEPs, peers and MPs should be set up which would meet from time to time – perhaps with specialized sub-committees – to discuss European policy.[2]

In Britain, and perhaps elsewhere, the further issue of relations between MEPs elected in Scotland and Wales and the devolved Assemblies will also arise. Some contact will no doubt be necessary and both the Assemblies and the MEPs – but perhaps not the central government! – are likely to find such links politically valu-

2. *Relations between the United Kingdom Parliament and the European Parliament after Direct Elections*, House of Lords Select Committee on the European Communities, Session 1977–78, 44th Report.

able. The Welsh and Scottish Labour Parties at any rate will be allowed considerable autonomy both in organization and in the formation of policy. It is interesting that the European Assembly Elections Act does not preclude the possibility of MEPs also being members of a devolved Assembly. Indeed, in its evidence to the Select Committee the SNP has proposed that MEPs elected in Scotland should have non-voting membership of the Scottish Assembly.

Whichever solutions are preferred – and as far as Westminster goes the responsibility lies on the House of Commons Committee on the Procedure and Practice of Parliament to come up with suggestions – it is clear that new and more complicated networks of political inter-relationships will be called into being by the directly elected EP. MEPs will face conflicting pressures and divided calls on their loyalties. One result may be the loosening of party disciplines, leaving MEPs with more personal freedom of action. Tight party groupings may give way to the looser coalitions of interest – producers versus consumers, 'haves' versus 'have-nots' – which are found in the Congress of the United States. But whatever happens it seems unlikely that the newly emerging European Party Organizations will be able to aspire to develop along the same lines as the tightly disciplined blocs that characterize the modern national political party systems in Europe. The centrifugal forces will be too powerful. No doubt the resultant of all the pressures will be something of a middle course.

Chapter 6: Towards European Union . . . ?

So far in this book our analysis has been essentially factual and descriptive. We know that direct elections will take place in June 1979 and every five years thereafter; we have been able to assess the development to date of the European Parliament and the Community system as a whole; we know what the electoral systems will be; and we can also foresee – indeed we can even predict with reasonable certainty – the political balance in the Parliament after the elections.

What we cannot do is to predict either the 'the sense of the House' or, at a more general level, what will be the future of the Community system of which the Parliament forms only a part. As for the Parliament itself, we cannot foresee what sort of balance of views will emerge around such issues as the extent of the Parliament's powers, its relations with the Commission and the Council, and the scope of the powers and responsibilities of the Community as such. Much will depend on such considerations as the kind of people who are elected to the Parliament, the internal politics of the member states, the way in which the world economic situation is seen to affect the Community and – last but by no means least – the impact of the 'enlargement' of the Community to include Greece, Portugal and Spain.

It must indeed be said that it is probably too early to be sure that the process of integration in the Community is irreversible. The election of the EP will impose yet another block – and an important one – in the way of regression. But even after direct elections the balance between national and supra-national elements in the Community's constitutional structure will still be uncertain, and 'enlargement' will increase the uncertainty. Is the future European Union to be more than another inter-governmental organization, at present only temporarily disguised? Or is the Community indeed developing as a novel form of political and economic association on a trans-national scale? On the one hand, in Britain, Denmark and France it emerged very strongly from the debates about direct elections that they were not regarded as the prelude to any radical institutional innovation in the Community in the near future.[1] On the other, current developments in the field of economic and monetary policy point towards a significant extension of the Community's powers and a strengthening of its institutions.

It seems to be the case that, over the years immediately ahead, there will be a continuing overall trend towards closer European unity, but that this will tend to happen without dramatic changes in the existing institutional arrangements. What we are likely to see is an organic and evolutionary process by which the existing structures of the Community continue to develop through successive cycles of challenge, response, consolidation – even regression – and rationalization. Policy, not institutions, will be in the lead: it will be the requirement to solve specific and concrete problems rather than the aspiration to perfect the Community's Constitution that will determine the pace and character of Europe's advance.

Continuity will be the watchword. The new Parliament will develop out of the old. Nevertheless, institutions have a life and logic of their own – a logic into which, in the case of the Community, a new factor will be introduced when a directly elected EP enters upon the European stage. Its principal immediate importance, at least in the authors' view, will not so much be to bring about progress itself, as to make progress possible – to supply the essential democratic pre-requisite for the further and keener pursuit of European solutions to Europe's problems. On this argument

1. In both Britain and France a provision was added to the legislation authorizing direct elections, specifying that any 'treaty' increasing the EP's powers would have to be approved by a positive legislative act of the national parliament. There is, however, a great deal of scope for the expansion of the EP's influence by such informal intra-institutional arrangements as the 'Joint Declaration' (see above, p. 71) which do not have the status of treaties. Any more far-reaching increase in the Parliament's powers would obviously be a development of first-class political importance, which would in any case require national assent.

the Community's future, and that of the European Parliament with it, is assured if it is indeed true that the scale of the problems Europe faces is essentially trans-national, and that the development of the Community's institutional logic towards deeper integration runs along the grain of our present and future problems.

What, then, will be the effect of the Community's push for successful solutions combined with the pull of the new Parliament?

The Parliament and the Commission

The Commission is commonly seen as the main focus of the EP's activities. And indeed it will be important for the Parliament to step up its scrutiny of the way in which the Commission uses its executive power and to increase its influence over the use which the Commission makes of its exclusive power of initiative.

When we analyse the relation between the Commission's executive role and the new EP we find a paradox which offers a key to understanding the effects of a directly elected EP on the Community's institutional system more generally. This is the paradox of democracy and the modern state: that the imposition of democratic accountability upon the executive power supplies the legitimacy which it needs to expand its authority. The effect upon the Commission of being held to account by the new EP will not so much be to check abuse – that is rarely the problem in modern government – as to make possible a growth in its activities, both legislative and executive. We will examine below how this 'democratic paradox' applies also to the Council; here the point is that after direct elections the Commission will be able to argue that its subjection to closer democratic scrutiny justifies the expansion of its executive role and the shift to it of executive powers at present largely wielded by member state officials remote from the scrutiny of any parliament.

The same type of argument applies in respect of the Commission's legislative role. Quite apart from the possibility discussed in Chapter 3 that the EP might acquire a right of initiative of its own, the EP's influence upon the Commission's use of its initiative power should both reinforce the Commission's ability to play its part in the Community's legislative process and enable the EP itself to develop an indirect power in that process. Positively, the EP's influence could be used to encourage the Commission to bring forward proposals it might otherwise regard as non-starters; we will consider below what effects its support in such cases might perhaps have upon the Council's decisions. Negatively, it might persuade the Commission to delay or refrain from putting a particular proposal on the table: indeed it might give the Commission a democratic authority for doing so even in cases – for example, in agriculture – where the Council is anxious to make a decision.

Would the efficacy of the Commission's initiative power be blunted if the EP were to acquire a right to have its resolutions considered by the Council? Almost certainly not: the Commission's initiative role does not come from a monopoly of conception – which it does not in fact possess – but from a monopoly of the right to formulate and amend specific legislative texts inside the Council. A right of initiative for the EP would not supplant the Commission's powers in this regard but would supplement them.[2] Meanwhile a potent weapon could be forged within the existing Treaty framework, if the right of initiative – with its implied veto power – were not duplicated but shared; that is if it were found to be constitutional and practicable for the Commission to refuse as a matter of course to put on the Council table proposals which lacked the endorsement of the Parliament.

For whether or not the EP acquires a formal right of initiative of its own – or a share in the nomination of the Commission or its President and perhaps a right to approve their programme – the really important questions in the relationship between the Commission and the EP will be how much support they can give one another. And here, although direct elections will increase the stature of the EP relative to the Commission – and there may be some

2. The same argument applies with regard to the EP's powers of initiative towards the Court of Justice. The EP already has the right to bring an action before the Court if the Council or the Commission *fail to* act in infringement of the Treaty. It might exercise this right; and it might also eventually be given further powers to approach the Court, equivalent to the powers of the Commission as the 'guardian of the Treaties'.

exciting incidents when the full-time Parliamentarians get to work – the underlying reality surely is that the relationship between the two institutions will be governed by their fundamental identity of interest in increasing the role of Community decision-making. However 'minimalist' the philosophy of many of those elected to the EP, they will probably find themselves impelled the other way by the logic of the position in which they will find themselves: they will be able to do their jobs properly only by making the Community work more effectively.

The Parliament and the Council

Because of the preponderance of the Council of Ministers in the Community institutional structure, for the time being the fulcrum of movement in the Community must lie in the Council. In the authors' view the effect of whatever progress the Community might make in the foreseeable future both will and should be not to diminish the Council's pre-eminence, but to make it easier for it to fulfil its functions as the Community's chief decision-making body.

At this stage in the development of the Community the weight of national consciousness greatly exceeds that of being European. In the absence of a widely shared sense of European citizenship and without a public opinion fully capable of understanding issues in European terms it is inevitable that the Council should operate more as a standing inter-governmental conference for reconciling conflicting national interests than as a Community institution guided principally by its sense of the European interest. And yet so long as this is the spirit which informs the Council it will be partially paralysed, rising but rarely and feebly to the level of the problems and the opportunities before it.

The European Council has emerged as one means of escaping this dilemma. The theory is that if the subordinate ministers cannot do it, then the definition of the common European interest must fall to the heads of government – who are of necessity those best placed in the national administrations to take a broad view. And perhaps also these regular meetings may help to draw public opinion in the member states towards a livelier awareness of European issues.

After nearly four years in operation the European Council seems to be proving its value as a means of helping the Council of Ministers to reach decisions. The resumption of progress in 1978 towards economic and monetary union has given dramatic evidence of the capacity of the European Council to provide a lead when it has the will. It seems clear that the directly elected EP will reinforce the efforts of the European Council to open up the European perspectives in which Community decisions must be made. As we saw in Chapter 3, the elections themselves, the Members working full-time – among other things to get themselves re-elected – the forging of inter-party links at the Community level, the creation at grass-roots level of political organizations with European goals, the use by the EP of the most up-to-date methods of mass communication: all of these things should have a cumulative effect upon public attitudes and aspirations. And against the background of the emergence and articulation of a stronger sense of European identity and citizenship it should be possible for the Council – if it so wishes – to fulfil with increasing effect its central role in the Community.

A more effective Council: what this means in practice is a Council which takes more decisions, which extends the range and depth of the Community's policy-making, which takes decisions in the longer-term interests of the whole Community rather than attending only to the balance of short-term national concerns. A bolder Council, a Council better able to rise above national pressures and constraints, a Council willing to lead . . . in short, a Council which will need the support of a directly representative European Parliament if it is not to exceed the limits of its own democratic legitimacy.

For the 'democratic paradox' whose effects upon the Commission we have already discussed also operates in relation to the Council, even though the Council in no sense resembles the Commission in being dependent upon the EP.

There is no doubt that the Council's effectiveness is diminished by what in Chapter 2 we called the 'accountability gap' which arises from the fact that the Council as such is not even indirectly accountable to any electorate. First, and perhaps most important, its ambitions are limited by the fragility and incoherence of the basis of its authority. Second, while its particular members may be severally accountable to their national legislatures, and through them individually to their national electorates, the Council as a body makes its decisions in secret and is accountable to no one. And the consequence of this lack of directly representative institutions at the European level is that the only way to save the Council for democracy is to maintain the possibility of the national veto – for, as we saw in Chapter 2, this provides, at least in theory, for the Council's negative accountability to the several national parliaments. Thus forms are saved, but at the expense of substance.

A directly elected Parliament can help the Council, if they both so will, to break through to greater effectiveness, by complementing the national parliaments as a basis of support, and by providing it for the first time with a democratic institutional partner at its own – that is the European – level. But how would that partnership work, and what would be its specific implications for the power of the EP – and for the national parliaments?

The essential feature of the partnership would be the support and the reinforced legitimacy which the decisions of a more effective Council could derive from the vote and voice of the elected EP.

Since a more effective Council is one which is able to respond to the Community's problems by expanding the range and depth of its policies, such an improvement is bound of itself to bring about an increase in the range of the EP's powers and influence. More ambitious Community policies entail more spending, which implies a natural 'horizontal' expansion of the scope of the EP's existing budgetary powers in the 'non-obligatory' sector. And new Community policies imply an equally natural 'horizontal' expansion of the field covered by the EP's powers of scrutiny and control and its existing legislative power of suspensory veto. The EP supports a more effective Council; a more effective Council widens the area of Community action; a wider sphere of Community action expands the influence of the EP.

All of this argument rests upon two principal assumptions: that the way forward is the way of integration; and that the member states in the Council will recognize this in the future as they have done in the past. These assumptions underlie the concept of a partnership between the Council and the EP; and through this natural interdependence they point to a formal extension in due course of the EP's legislative and budgetary powers.

The greater the range and weight of the problems which the Council seeks to solve – and problems press in regardless of our appetite for solving them – the more it will need the support of the EP. Further, the more it improves its capacity to make decisions by attenuating the operation of the national veto, the greater will be its requirement for a European source of democratic legitimacy: it is no accident that the powers of the EP are most developed in the budgetary sphere where majority voting in the Council has become the rule. But the more the Council looks to the EP for support in wider matters of policy the clearer will be the weakness of the latter's powers over legislation – for a power of refusal that does not bind is a power of assent that has little effect.

Thus there will naturally emerge a demand for strengthening the EP as a partner for the Council; and this can only be done by going up the hierarchy of legislative powers outlined in Chapter 3, first to increase the time over which the EP's suspensory veto may operate, and then to confer upon it a power of co-decision or final veto. Only the highest power in the hierarchy must under the present constitutional arrangements remain beyond its reach – the power of passing positively binding resolutions: for such a power would fundamentally transform the relationship between the Council and the parliaments of the member states.

The European Parliament and the National Parliaments

So we are brought directly to the question of the relationship between the EP and the national parliaments.

As we saw in Chapter 3, within the existing institutional framework whose future evolution we are considering, there can be no question of the EP determining the composition of the Council. Although it means that there exists no democratic way of changing the composition of the Council as a body – the centre of decision in the Community is therefore a form of standing coalition – the choice of the Council's several members remains a function for the various national parliaments or electorates to which they are severally responsible.

The limits which this implies for the development of the EP's powers are clear. The Parliament may find the Council guilty, but it cannot hope to pass sentence. Above all, it can pass resolutions addressed to the Council, but it cannot hope to see them positively binding upon it.

It can, however, hope to be able to say 'no'. For the extension into the legislative sphere of the power of final veto which the EP already has over the 'non-obligatory' sector of the budget does not by itself diminish the powers of the national parliaments. Here the crucial question is in fact not so much that of the expansion of the EP's legislative role as that of the way in which the Council makes its decisions: so long as it decides by unanimity, the legislative powers of the EP and those of the national parliaments are in essence complementary – one veto cannot contradict another, but can only reinforce it. But, when the Council decides by vote, in whatever form, the national parliaments in effect lose their power of control and only the EP can replace them.

There can be no disguising the fact that the EP stands to gain on every score by the further attenuation of the practice of unanimity in the Council; and it is also true, as we argued above, that the existence of a directly elected representative partner should make it easier for the Council – if it so chooses – to operate less inflexibly. Nevertheless, the argument about the Council's decision-making procedures – although first of all a question between governments – is not so much an issue between the EP and the national parliaments as a question between the Council and the national parliaments to which its members are severally responsible.

There is, however, no doubt that there exists a sense of rivalry in the attitude of some national parliamentarians towards the prospect of a directly elected EP. And this is clearly connected with questions of power and jurisdiction, at the heart of which lies the national veto: the essential instrument by which – in theory at least – the national parliaments assert the Council's negative accountability to them.

It should be remembered that since 1974 the Council has already begun to make its decisions more flexibly. But since the question of how much further it should go in this direction is of some importance to the future relationship between the EP and the national parliaments, the question needs to be considered whether in practice the national veto really can work as an instrument of accountability. As our argument draws to a conclusion this question has the added merit of returning us to the intractable ground of reality upon which all principles of government must be tested.

How much control do national parliaments in fact exercise over the Council? The answer is, in effect, very little. Some national parliaments, such as the French National Assembly, are constitutionally and politically debarred from exercising such control. Others, such as the Dutch parliament and the German Bundestag, exert sporadic but only occasionally effective control through the use of their normal procedures for influencing the policy of their executives – but at the same time they tend to consider that stronger national parliamentary control over Community policy could have damaging effects on the Community's development. Only in the three new member states has a real effort been made to provide for a measure of day-to-day parliamentary scrutiny of the governments' doings in Europe, and these efforts have met with mixed success. The Danish parliament alone – whose 'Market Relations Committee' in effect mandates ministers – has succeeded in devising a workable and effective system, but, as can be seen in Appendix C (pp. 164–5 below), it is a system that only works because of special factors unique to Denmark – and it is distinctly not for export.

In the British House of Commons, although there is widespread dissatisfaction with the way in which the Select Committee on European Legislation is working, any serious attempts at reform are likely to come up against the traditional reluctance of the House to delegate real powers to its Committees. And, more fundamentally, the drive to enforce the Commons' control of government policy clashes with the concept of the executive's responsibility for external policy, subject to the overall confidence of the House. As we saw in Chapter 2, all governments see the Community's Council of Ministers as a forum for negotiation and bargaining, and precisely because the issues at stake involve important national interests they will normally fend off every attempt of the national parliaments to impose real constraints upon them – unless it is a question of finding an alibi, if that is what they seek, for failing to reach agreement with their partners.

In fact, the control that the national parliaments are sometimes able to assert is more political than constitutional, more a matter of influence than of the assertion of formal powers. This is a control which generally operates by limiting the horizons of the governments sitting in the Council, by restricting their ambitions and constraining their sense of what is possible. And if this might indeed be conceived as a remote form of accountability, its effect is not so much to determine the fate of particular measures as to weaken the overall capacity of the Council to act effectively.

The loss which comes of this is not the Council's only. For if the Community, acting through the Council, cannot rise to the level of its problems those problems will most likely go unresolved. The sovereignty over events which we fail to capture at the Community level does not automatically accrue to the member states and their parliaments: it is lost altogether. And the very purpose for which the Community was created – that its members should recapture together the power which escapes them separately – is denied.

It would, however, be wrong to over-state the extent to which the national parliaments and the EP may be or become rivals for power. The deficiencies in the EP's powers, together with the ineffectiveness in practice of parliamentary control over the executives at the national level, point rather towards a close alliance between a set of institutions each of which is seeking from a weak position to reassert the possibility of a real measure of control by representative parliaments over executives which are everywhere and at every level more dominant. When that dominance arises because the executive has responded more readily to the needs of the times – and this is, after all, the essential responsibility of the executive – parliamentarians are bound to consider whether they too must not find new ways of doing their business: including the possibility of going European.

Appendix A: Political Parties in the Member States

BELGIUM

Belgium has a bicameral parliament, including a Chamber of Representatives with 212 members. The government at the time of writing is formed by a coalition based on the Christian Democrats and the Socialists – PSC/CVP plus PSB/BSP plus VU plus FDR.

From left to right the main parties are:

Communists (PCB/KPB). Small and rather old-fashioned, its support lies only in Brussels and French-speaking Wallonia. In the 1977 elections it won 2·7 per cent of the votes, giving it 3 seats.

Socialists (PSB/BSP). Founded in 1885, it is essentially a Social Democratic Party. Its main support lies in Wallonia where it got 39·4 per cent of the vote in 1977. It has always favoured a unitary Belgian state, and it has close relations with the trade-union movement. It has been in government for thirty-nine years since 1915. Its leading figures are André Cools and Henri Simonet. In the 1977 elections it won 26·8 per cent of the vote and 59 seats.

Christian Democrats (PSC/CVP). The two linguistic wings of the party have been at odds over regionalization since 1968. It is a moderate centre party, mainly Catholic, with strong trade-union and leftist links in Wallonia. In Flanders it is more conservative. It is the dominant party in Belgian politics; and it has been in government for fifty-six years since 1916. It has its main strength in Flanders, where it won 43·9 per cent of the vote in 1977. In the 1977 elections it took 35·9 per cent of the overall vote, giving it 72 seats. Its leading figures are Leo Tindemans – the former Prime Minister of Belgium – Charles-Fernand Nothomb and Wilfrid Martens.

Liberals (PRLW/PVV). The Wallon wing is more regionalist and more centrist, having been reinforced by ex-Rassemblement Wallon members in 1976. It has strong links with industry. Traditionally a lay party, it is now, however, less anti-Catholic. As a party it has been losing ground since the mid-1960s; nevertheless since 1945 it has been in government for some fourteen years. In the 1977 elections it won 14·4 per cent of the vote, or 30 seats. Its main leaders are Willy de Clercq and Paul Damseaux.

Rassemblement Wallon (RW). This is a small left-of-centre regionalist party in Wallonia. It split in 1976. In the 1977 elections it won 9·10 per cent of the vote, standing in Wallonia only. This gave it 5 seats.

Front Démocratique des Francophones (FDF). This is the Brussels French language defence party in Brussels founded in 1964. In the 1977 elections it won 34·9 per cent of the vote in Brussels, giving it 10 seats. Its leader is Mme Antoinette Spaak, daughter of the former Socialist Prime Minister.

Volksunie (VU). This is a Flemish nationalist party which seeks a Flemish state. In economic and social terms it is rather conservative. It was founded in 1954. In the 1977 elections it won 10·9 per cent of the vote – 16·5 per cent of the vote in Flanders, and 20 seats. Its leader is Hugo Schilz.

DENMARK

Denmark has a unicameral parliament, or Folketing, with 179 members. At the time of writing the Social Democrats are conducting a minority government.

The main parties are:

Danish Communist Party (DKP). This is a small party which split after internal dissension over the Soviet invasion of Hungary in 1956. It had no members in the Folketing between 1960–73. In the 1977 election it won 3·7 per cent of the votes, gaining 7 seats.

Socialist Peoples' Party (SF). It broke away from DKP in 1956, led by the then General Secretary of the DKP, Aksel Larsen. Its supporters are mainly intellectuals. It soon supplanted the DKP as the leading 'left-wing' ginger-group opposed to NATO and the EEC. In the 1977 election it won 35 per cent of the vote, with 7 seats. Its leader is Gert Petersen.

Left Socialists (VS). This is a small 'New Left' breakaway from SF, after a split in 1968. It has taken up a variety of direct-action causes – for instance in opposition to nuclear energy. It is anti-EEC, but internationalists. In 1977 its share of the poll was 2·7 per cent, giving it 5 seats.

Social Democrats. The party was founded in the 1890s. It draws its strength mainly from the cities, but it has significant support all over the country. In essence it is a moderate reformist Social Democratic Party, stressing economic growth and high levels of welfare. There is an active anti-EEC minority. Since the 1920s it has been the dominant party in Denmark. At the 1977 elections it won 37·1 per cent of the vote and 65 seats. Its leading personality is Anker Jørgensen.

Radical Party (RV). It originated at the beginning of the century as a peasant/small farmer party and it is still essentially an alliance of intellectuals and small farmers. It has a strong neutralist and pacifist wing which led it to oppose Danish entry into NATO. It thus has an important anti-EEC minority. It left the European Liberal Federation in 1978 because its programme was not radical enough. In the spectrum of Danish politics it is just to the right of the Social Democrats, with which it has been a frequent coalition partner. In 1977 it won 3·6 per cent of the vote and 7 seats.

Conservatives (KF). This is the traditional moderate right-wing party with close links to industry and its base among the white-collar workers, the independent tradesmen and larger farmers. It is strongly pro-EEC. It has participated in many centre-right coalitions, and is at present recovering from a disastrous decline in the early 1970s. In 1977 it won 8·5 per cent of the vote and 15 seats.

Centre Democrats (CD). This party broke from the Social Democrats in 1973 over its alleged 'leftist' tendencies. It is a moderate party which supports the EEC; together with the KF it sits with the British Conservatives in the EP's Conservative Group. In 1977 it won 6·4 per cent of the vote and 11 seats.

Christian Peoples' Party (KrF). This is not like the other continental Christian Democratic Parties and it is not a member of the European Peoples' Party. It was founded in 1971 in protest against pornography and abortion law reforms. It has been described as 'culturally conservative and socially leftish'. In 1977 it won 3·4 per cent of the vote, and 6 seats.

Progress Party. This is the anti-tax and anti-bureaucracy party founded by Mogens Glistrup. It grew like wildfire after its establishment in 1973, but seems now to have reached a plateau. It has taken votes from all parties, but its impact in the Folketing has been almost nil. It split in 1974. In 1977 it won 14·6 per cent of the vote, and 26 seats.

Justice Party. This is a party based on the single-tax theories of Henry George; it is ultra-liberal and committed to free trade. It is opposed to the EEC. In 1977 it won 3·3 per cent of the votes and 6 seats.

FRANCE

France has a bicameral legislature within a presidential system of government. The Lower House, the National Assembly, has 490 Members.

The main parties are:

Communist Party (PCF). Formed after the scission of the Socialist Party at the Congress of Tours in 1920, it has been slower than the Italian Communist Party to de-Stalinize. Nevertheless it has accepted French membership of NATO and the EEC. It has a strong working-class electorate and it has kept a constant 20 per cent share of the vote since 1945. It participated in government coalitions between 1944 and 1947. In the (second round of the)

1978 elections it won 18·6 per cent of the vote and 86 seats. Its leader is Georges Marchais.

Socialist Party. After the low point of the 1969 Presidential election, when it won only 5 per cent of the votes, the party has been totally renewed in leadership, policies, organization and membership. It is now a 'broad church': marxist to social democrat. Its left-wing is opposed to the supra-national development of the EEC. Since 1972 it has been in alliance with the PCF and MRG in the so-called 'Union of the Left' which failed to win a majority in the Assembly elections of 1978. This has unleashed a wide internal debate about the party's future alignments. In the 1978 elections it won 28·3 per cent of the votes and 103 seats. Its leader is François Mitterand.

Left-Wing Radicals (MRG). This party broke away from the mainstream Radicals in 1972 to join the Union of the Left. It represents the survival of the traditional anti-clerical, 'républicain' radicalism of the Midi and South-West. In 1978 it won 2·3 per cent of the votes and 10 seats. Its new leader is Michel Crépeau.

Union pour la Démocratie Française (UDF). This is a new political formation which was established shortly before the March 1978 National Assembly elections. It comprises the non-Gaullist forces of the 'Majority', and represents President Giscard's electoral base. It is reformist and more pro-EEC than the Gaullists. In effect it is a Union of the old Parti Républicain, the Centristes and the Radicals. In 1978 it won 23·1 per cent of the votes and 137 seats.

Rassemblement pour la République (RPR). The RPR is the new name for the Gaullist Party. It was formed by Jacques Chirac in 1976. Gaullism is a nationalist, classless, social and even populist, but at times authoritarian movement. It dislikes classification as either 'right' or 'left'. It was opposed to direct elections. In 1978 it won 26·1 per cent of the votes and 148 seats.

GERMANY

Germany has a bicameral federal system in which the Lower House is the 596-member Bundestag. Since 1969 it has been ruled by a Social Democrat–Liberal coalition.

The main parties are:

Social Democrats (SPD). This has an old and distinguished pre-war tradition. Since its adoption of the Bad Godesberg programme in 1958 it has repudiated Marxism. It accepts the principles of a market economy, and it is firmly committed to the EEC. After 1969 it was the architect of West Germany's *Ostpolitik*, or opening to the East. Its leaders are Helmut Schmidt and Willy Brandt. In 1976 it won 42·6 per cent of the vote and 214 seats.

Christian Democratic Union (CDU/CSU). This was founded after the last war and it was the main government party until 1969. The CDU wing is moderate and has close trade union links in the Rhineland. The CSU (in Bavaria) of Franz-Josef Strauss is more right-wing – a law and order party. In 1976 it won 48·6 of the vote and 243 seats. The CDU/CSU's leaders are Helmut Kohl and F.-J. Strauss.

Free Democrats (FDP). This is the German Liberal Party. In the 1950s the FDP occupied a position to the right of the CDU/CSU – it was a classic 'economic' liberal party. However it underwent a change in the 1960s. It is disproportionately influential because of its permanent 'swing' position: it was in government in partner-ship with the CDU/CSU from 1949 to 1966 and with the SPD after 1969. In 1976 it won 7·9 per cent of the vote and 39 seats. Its leader is Hans-Dietrich Genscher.

IRELAND

Ireland has a bicameral legislature. The Lower House is the 155-member Dail Eireann. Since 1977 the government has been formed by the Fianna Fail.

The main parties are:

Labour. Labour was founded in 1912, but took part in its first election in 1922. It has always had a mixture of support both from Dublin and from rural areas. It is a moderate party which has always avoided conflict with Ireland's strong Catholic traditions. It has never quite taken off – its best result was in 1922 when it won 21·1 per cent of the votes. It governed in coalition with Fine Gail in 1954–7 and 1973–7. In 1977 it won 11·6 per cent of the first-preference votes and 17 seats.

Fine Gail. The main Irish parties originated in the events of the Irish Revolution. In the 1920s FG was the 'moderate' nationalist faction, favouring the Treaty with Britain. Since it went into opposition in 1977 it has experienced a renewal and it is now becoming more of a 'social democratic' party. In 1977 it won 30·4 per cent of the first-preference votes and 43 seats. Its leader is Garret Fitzgerald.

Fianna Fail. FF was de Valera's party – the hard-line Republican faction in the civil war period in the 1920s. It has always been more nationalist than FG and perhaps more populist, with support from all over Ireland. Since 1977 there have been some signs of an ideological clarification of Irish politics and FF has tended to shift to the right. Its 1977 victory was of unprecedented dimensions. At that election it won 50·6 per cent of the first-preference votes and 84 seats. Its leader is Jack Lynch, the present Prime Minister.

ITALY

The Italian parliament has two co-equal chambers, the lower house being a Chamber of Deputies with 630 Members. The present government consists of Christian Democrats ruling on a minority basis with support from five other parties including the Communists.

The main parties are:

Communist Party (PCI). This is the Community's largest Communist party. It is committed to 'eurocommunism' and 'pluralist democracy'. It supports Italy's membership both of the EEC and of NATO and it is critical of the Soviet Union. For some three years it has indirectly supported DC governments under the doctrine of the 'Historic Compromise'. In 1976 it won 34·4 per cent of the votes and 226 seats. Its leader is Enrico Berlinguer.

Italian Socialist Party (PSI). This small party has at times in the last five years seemed more radical than the PCI, although since 1963 it has participated in governments with the DC. This has in reality gravely compromised its working-class support and its overall credibility. In 1976 it won 9·6 per cent of the votes and 57 seats. Its leader is Bettino Craxi.

Italian Social Democratic Party (PSDI). This is a small and conservative social democratic party, anti-Communist, with a lower middle-class electoral clientele. Since 1963 it has taken part in a series of centre-left governments. Its future must now be in doubt. In 1976 it won 3·4 per cent of the votes and 15 seats.

Christian Democrats (DC). The Christian Democrats have been in government since the end of the war. In the 1950s they even obtained an absolute majority. It is a broad popular party with a left wing which is close to the trade unions and a right wing close to the Church. In recent years it seems to have suffered from a kind of paralysis and a series of scandals, but has shown a remarkable capacity for survival and, indeed, now seems to be recovering ground lost in 1976. In 1976 it won 38·7 per cent of the votes and 262 seats. Its leader, the present Prime Minister, is Giulio Andreotti.

Republican Party. This is a small lay party, which has inherited part of the non-Socialist lay middle-class electorate. Its influence has depended more on the personality of its leader, Ugo La Malfa, than on electoral strength. It has participated in a series of centre-left governments since the early 1960s. In 1976 it won 3·1 per cent of the votes and 14 seats.

Liberal Party (PLI). The PLI is a right-wing Liberal Party, close to business interests, and without a great deal of electoral support. It has at times – most recently in 1972 – been a partner for the DC when it wished to form a centre-right coalition. It is now in severe decline. It is part of the family of Italian lay parties, and it supported divorce and abortion. In 1976 it won only 1·3 per cent of the votes and 5 seats.

Italian Right Social Movement (DN-MSI). The DN-MSI was formed in the early 1970s from the fusion of the neo-Fascist MSI

(Italian Social Movement) and the Monarchist Party. Its high point was the 1972 election when it won 8·7 per cent of the votes – although in earlier elections the two parties had between them obtained as much as 12·6 per cent. It is anti-Communist and anti-parliamentary, authoritarian and nationalist, nostalgic for the Fascist period. In 1976 its share of the vote fell to 6·1 per cent, giving it 35 seats.

LUXEMBOURG

Luxembourg has a unicameral legislature with 52 members. The government is formed by a Labour-Socialist coalition.

The main parties are:

Communist Party (PCL). This is the third largest Communist party in the Community in terms of its share of the vote. Its support is concentrated in the steel industry workers in the south of the country. It is not a 'Euro-communist' party. In 1974 it won 10·4 per cent of the votes and 5 seats.

Socialists (PSOL). This is a moderate, anti-clerical party. It suffered a split in the early 1970s. In 1974 it won 29·1 per cent of the vote and 17 seats.

Christian Social Party. A Christian Democrat Party, it has a populist wing which would prefer coalition with the PSOL to coalition with the PD. It is generally the largest party in Luxembourg. In 1974 it won 28·0 per cent of the vote and 17 seats.

Democratic Party. This is the Luxembourg Liberal Party, led by the Prime Minister, Gaston Thorn. In 1974 it won 22·1 per cent of the vote and 13 seats.

THE NETHERLANDS

The Netherlands has a bicameral legislature, with a Lower House of 150 members. Since 1977 it has been governed by a Christian Democrat-Labour coalition.

The main parties are:

Labour (Pvd A). Founded in 1894, it has never won more than the 33·8 per cent share of the vote that it obtained in 1977. In the 1960s and early 1970s it took on board ideas from the New Left and ecological movements, becoming more radical. It has been attempting to form a progressive bloc with three other small parties, to give more coherence to the fragmented Dutch political system. In 1977 it won 53 seats.

Christian Democratic Appeal (CDA). The CDA was formed in 1976 as a united Christian Party made up of two small Protestant parties – which are rather right-wing – and the more centrist Catholic Party, the largest of the three. Its electorate lies mostly in the south and rural areas. In 1977 it won 31·9 per cent of the votes and 49 seats. Its leader is the present Prime Minister, Andreas van Agt.

Freedom Party (VVD). This is the Dutch Liberal Party. The VVD is to the right in the political spectrum, but of late it has become more pragmatic. In 1977 it won 17·9 per cent of the votes and 28 seats.

Democrats 66 (D'66). A new small party which was formed in the turbulent atmosphere of Dutch politics in the 1960s. Its objective has been to modernize and streamline the political system. It is allied to the PvdA. In 1977 it won 5·4 per cent of the votes and 6 seats.

THE UNITED KINGDOM

Britain has a bicameral legislature. The Upper House is part hereditary, part nominated. The Lower Chamber – the House of Commons – has 630 members. The government has been formed by the Labour Party since the October 1974 election.

The main parties are:

Labour Party. Founded by the trade unions at the beginning of the century, this is a broad-based party of social democrats, trade-unionists and marxists. Its support comes mainly from the declining industrial areas of the North of England, Scotland and Wales.

Since 1976 it has governed with the support of the Liberals. At the 1974 election it won 39·2 per cent of the votes and 319 seats. Its leader is Mr James Callaghan.

The Liberal Party. This is the descendant of the party of Gladstone and Asquith. Its supporters come mainly from a protest vote against the two main parties. At the election it won 18·3 per cent of the votes and 13 seats. Its present leader is David Steel.

Conservatives. This is the party of Peel and Disraeli, of Edward Heath and Margaret Thatcher. It tries to be the party of the 'whole nation' but it risks becoming the party of the more prosperous southern part of England. At the 1974 election it won 35·8 per cent of the votes and 277 seats. Its leader is Mrs Margaret Thatcher.

Scottish Nationalist Party (SNP). The SNP broke through to prominence in the late 1960s after several decades on the 'lunatic fringe' of politics. It has now almost succeeded in attaining its minimum objective of Home Rule for Scotland. Its future is uncertain. At the 1974 election it won 30·4 per cent of the vote (in Scotland only) and 11 seats (out of 71).

Plaid Cymry (PC). Hopes to emulate the SNP, in Wales. It won 10·8 per cent of the votes in 1974 (Wales only), and 3 seats (out of 36).

Appendix B: Electoral Systems in the Nine – National and European

Country	National electoral system	European Parliament electoral system
Belgium	Provincial lists: multi-member constituencies, which, except for Brussels, are unilingual.	A Flemish (13 seats) constituency and a Walloon (11 seats) constituency. Brussels voters may vote for either one of the lists.
Denmark	135 MPs elected in small multi-member constituencies, using the modified Sainte-Laguë rule. 40 supplementary seats make up proportion for the small parties. 2 per cent exclusion rule.*	One 15-member national constituency, using the D'hondt rule. List alliances allowed. Greenland returns one member.
Germany	Half the Bundestag members are elected in single-member seats by plurality vote. The other half (to realize proportionality) are elected from *Land* lists. 5 per cent exclusion rule.	Parties may choose a *Land* list or national list. 5 per cent exclusion rule.*
France	490 seats in Metropolitan France and overseas. Single-member seats. Second ballot is held in seats where no candidate obtains an absolute majority on the first ballot.	National list with 10 per cent exclusion rule.

Country	National electoral system	European Parliament electoral system
Ireland	3, 4 or 5 member seats. STV used.*	3, 4, 5 member seats based on four Provincial constituencies. STV.
Italy	Regional multi-member constituencies, using the Imperiali system; second distribution of surplus votes in national pool on largest remainder method, if any seats remain.	No decision yet: expected to be a regional list system with up to eight constituencies.
Luxembourg	4 multi-member constituencies. PR used.	Probably two constituencies with PR list system.
Netherlands	In effect one national constituency for all 150 Second Chamber seats, with a basic quota fixed for winning one seat.	One national constituency.
United Kingdom	630 single-member constituencies. First past the post.	78 single-member constituencies in England (66), Wales (4) and Scotland (8). One 3-seat constituency in Northern Ireland, where STV will be used.

*exclusion rule: percentage of vote below which a party gains no seats.
STV – Single Transferable Vote.

Appendix C: The Role of National Parliaments in Community Affairs – the Danish Example

The Danish Folketing's Market Relations Committee (MRC) was set up in 1961 to monitor the negotiations for Danish entry to the EEC. In 1973, after accession, it became the agent of the Danish parliament in exercising day-to-day control over Danish Ministers in respect of Community affairs. At that time the system which applies today – with minor refinements – was laid down.

The government makes available, with its comments, all Commission proposals. These may be sent by the MRC to other specialist parliamentary committees for an opinion. At its weekly meeting (usually held on a Friday) the MRC goes through every item of business arising on the Council agenda over the next week. The Minister concerned indicates the government's intended position.

The Committee may then discuss this position. If there is no majority against it the Minister has a 'mandate' and can proceed. Were a majority to form against him he would have to modify his position so as to satisfy the Committee.

No votes are taken. The Chairman takes the 'sense of the meeting'. He does so by counting up the strength represented on the floor of the Chamber behind each party spokesman. If, in the course of negotiations in Brussels, the Minister is faced with new proposals, he must once again consult the MRC, if necessary by telephone and in the person of its Chairman. This may happen at any time of the night, at weekends, or out of session.

The MRC is a political, not a technical Committee. Its seventeen members and ten 'alternates' are chosen by the House to reflect its political make-up. The MRC's members are always leading party figures – former Ministers, senior party spokesmen – who have the prestige to commit their parties in confidential discussions without prior consultation. This is an essential element in the procedure: for the MRC's conclusions must be confidential, swiftly arrived at, and morally and politically binding on the parties.

The MRC is the most far-reaching example of national parliamentary control over Community affairs. However, all the evidence tends to show that this system, if it is suitable for Denmark, is not exportable – least of all to Westminster. It rests first of all on a different parliamentary tradition from that of Westminster. The Danish parliament only adopted a system of specialized committees in 1971, but, unlike Westminster, had nonetheless traditionally given 'delegated' powers of decision to certain important committees. The MRC has fitted quite easily into this tradition of powerful committees. In effect it takes decisions which are binding upon the political parties and therefore upon the whole House.

There is also in Denmark a long tradition of parliamentary involvement in the making of foreign policy, based upon close and confidential discussions between the government and a parliamentary committee. Here again, the MRC is operating within normal Danish parliamentary traditions which have no analogy at Westminster.

Moreover, it should be remembered that there is an element of 'complicity' with government in the Danish arrangements. While it is true that the government must submit to a mandate from the MRC (in fact it can do much to formulate the mandate in an acceptable manner), it benefits in return from the security of the Committee's support. The effect is that, provided it complies with the established procedures, it becomes immune from serious political criticism. In this way the anti-marketeers and the whole range of opposition parties are 'co-opted' and criticism is defused. It is very doubtful that such procedures – however sensible – would be acceptable at Westminster.

For a study of how the Westminster system for the scrutiny of Community business works – or fails to work – see Harris N. Miller, 'The Influence of British Parliamentary Committees on European Communities Legislation' in *Legislative Studies Quarterly*, II, 1, February 1977.

Appendix D: Salaries and Allowances of Members

	Annual salary	Ratio of salary to average national salary	Research and secretarial expenses and resources available
Belgium	1,310,000 BF (£22,200)	Figures not available	Subsidy of 200,000 BF (£3,300 per member) payable to each party group in Parliament. Free inland telephone service. Free stationery and postage (limited).
Denmark	131,806 DKr (£12,800)	Figures not available	Subsidy of about 45,000 DKr (£4,370) per member per annum is paid to each party for research and secretarial expenses. Free stationery. Free inland telephone service from the Folketing.
Federal Republic of Germany	*Bundestag* (Lower House): DM 90,000 (£23,800) *Bundesrat* (Upper House): No salary	Approximately 3¾ times the average national salary (DM 2,015 per month)	Bundestag (Lower House) has a Library and Press Documentation Centre, with a total of about 100 staff to provide research services for Deputies. Free postage.

# of Parliament of the Nine

Expense allowances	*Office space and accommodation available*	*Recreational and social facilities*
Free inland bus and train travel. Reduction for flights within Belgian territory. No private car allowances.	Members do not have individual offices; they can use Parliament library or party offices.	
Annual subsistence allowance of between 12,300 Kr (£1,190) and 36,200 Kr (£3,510) depending on distance of constituency from Copenhagen. Free inland bus, rail, ferry and air travel.	Most members have a room each.	
DM 54,000 (£14,300) per annum to cover: (a) subsistence (b) complete upkeep of office outside Bundestag (c) care of constituency (d) official travel within the FRG	Fully equipped office provided in Bundestag for each deputy.	Bundestag (Lower House) has a sports club, with football and tennis facilities.

	Annual salary	Ratio of salary to average national salary	Research and secretarial expenses and resources available
France	FF 192,180 (£22,880)	Figures not available	FF 5,300 (£640) per month for a Secretary and FF 4,200 (£500) for an assistant. Free stationery and postage. Free inland telephone service from Parliament. Quota of free calls from a member's home.
Italy	16,578,950 lire (£10,450)	Figures not available	Salary ('indemnity') specifically includes research and secretarial expenses. Free local telephone service.
Luxembourg	Fr. Lux. 288,800 (£4,900)	Figures not available	Secretarial allowance of Fr. Lux. 83,000 (£1,400) per member, payable to parties. Free telephone service from parliamentary building.
The Netherlands	*Second Chamber:* (Deputies) Fl. 85,000 (£21,250)	*Second Chamber:* Three times the national average	*Second Chamber:* Allowances of Fl. 18,000 (£4,500) per annum for a Secretary/ Assistant. Free telephone services from the parliamentary buildings. Free postage.

Expense allowances	*Office space and accommodation available*	*Recreational and social facilities*
Residual allowance of FF 1,190 (£140) per month. Free rail travel. Eighty free air journeys to constituency and eight journeys within French territory per annum. Loans provided at privileged rates to buy houses and flats.	Separate offices for each representative in National Assembly.	Sports and recreation hall. Sauna.
Subsistence allowance of 3,240,000 lire (£2,050) per annum. Seventy free return trips from constituency to Parliament, by public transport. Free rail travel at all times.	Office space is provided for members who hold particular offices in either house.	Restaurant and bar services in each house.
Free travel within the Grand-Duchy. Travel costs reimbursed.	Each political party has one office and one secretary at its disposal.	
Second Chamber: Subsistence allowance of Fl.9,373–18,746 (£2,300–£4,600). Travel expenses for journeys between home and Parliament.	*Second Chamber:* Offices in the Parliament building.	Gymnasium. Restaurant, coffee rooms and bar.

	Annual salary	Ratio of salary to average national salary	Research and secretarial expenses and resources available
	First Chamber: (Senators) No salary. Daily allowance for each day that the Chamber meets of between Fl. 94 (£23) and Fl. 187 (£46) depending on distance from place of residence to The Hague.		*First Chamber:* Library, documentation section and typing pool available.
United Kingdom	*House of Commons:* £6,270	Figures not available	*House of Commons:* Allowance of up to £3,687 per annum for secretarial or research assistance and other expenses. Free stationery. Free inland postage and telephone service.

Source: House of Commons Written Answers, 4 May 1978.

Expense allowances	*Office space and accommodation available*	*Recreational and social facilities*

First Chamber:
Fl.6,365 (£1,590) per annum travel expenses. Fl.3,893 (£970) per annum for other expenses. Hotel expenses in The Hague are paid for.

First Chamber:
Each political group has one room available for meetings etc.

House of Commons:
Subsistence allowance of up to £2,534 per annum if the member has to stay away from home. Allowance of £385 per annum for London members. Repayment of fare or car (average allowance 13·4 pence per mile for all journeys between home and Westminster and within constituencies).

There are 254 single rooms available (80 of these for Ministers), out of a total of 673 writing places allocated to members.

Gymnasium in Houses of Parliament.

Further Reading

BIEBER, R., and PALMER, M. (1976). 'A Community Without a Capital', *Journal of Common Market Studies*, 15:1–8.

COCKS, SIR B. (1973). *The European Parliament*. London: HMSO.

COOMBES, D. (1970). *Politics and Bureaucracy in the European Community*. London: Allen & Unwin.

COOMBES, D., and others (1976). *The Power of the Purse*. London: Allen & Unwin.

EHLERMANN, C.-D. (1975). 'Applying the New Budgetary Procedure for the First Time (Article 203 of the EEC Treaty)', *Common Market Law Review*, 12:325–43.

FITZMAURICE, J. (1975). *The Party Groups in the European Parliament*. Farnborough: Saxon House.

FITZMAURICE, J. (1978). *The European Parliament*. Farnborough: Saxon House.

HENIG, S. (1973–4a). 'New Institutions for European Integration', *Journal of Common Market Studies*, 12:130–37.

HENIG, S. (1973–4b). 'The Institutional Structure of the European Communities', *Journal of Common Market Studies*, 12:373–409.

HERMAN, V. (1976). *Parliaments of the World: A Reference Compendium*. London: Macmillan.

HERMAN, V., and LODGE, J. (1978). *The European Parliament and the European Community*. London: Macmillan.

KAPTEYN, P. J. G. (1972). 'The European Parliament, the Budget, and Legislation in the Community', *Common Market Law Review*, 9:386–410.

NOEL, E. (1973). 'The Commission's Power of Initiative', *Common Market Law Review*, 10:123–36.

PALMER, M. (1977). 'The Role of a Directly Elected European Parliament', *The World Today*, 33:122–30.

SCHWED, J. J. (1970). 'Les Questions écrites du Parlement Européen à la Commission', *Revue du Marché Commun*, 135:365–8.

SPINELLI, A. (1966). *The Eurocrats*. Baltimore: Johns Hopkins.

STRASSE, D. (1975). 'La Nouvelle Procédure budgetaire des Communautés Européennes et son application à l'établissment du budget pour l'exercise 1975', *Revue du Marché Commun*, 182:74–87.

VEDEL, G. L. (1975). 'The Role of the Parliamentary Institution in European Integration', in Directorate General for Research and Documentation of the European Parliament, ed., *Symposium on European Integration and the Future of Parliaments in Europe*. Luxembourg: European Parliament.

WHEARE, K. C. (1968). *Legislatures*, 2nd ed. London: Oxford University Press.